WISDOM OF THE EAST

THE BUDDHA'S
"WAY OF VIRTUE"

A TRANSLATION OF THE DHAMMAPADA
FROM THE PALI TEXT

BY W. D. C. WAGISWARA

AND

K. J. SAUNDERS

MEMBERS OF THE ROYAL ASIATIC SOCIETY, CEYLON BRANCH

British Library Cataloguing-in-Publication Data
A catalogue record for this book is available from
the British Library

THE BUDDHA'S
"WAY OF VIRTUE"

.

THE BUDDHIST IDEAL

" ' Eschew all evil : cherish good : cleanse your inmost thoughts '—this is the teaching of Buddhas."

Dhammapada, 183.

" Everything has two handles, the one by which it may be carried, the other by which it may not. . . . Lay hold of the handle by which it can be carried."

EPICTETUS (*Encheiridion* xliii).

TO

N. P. C.

REJOICE at the glad tidings! Buddha, our Lord, has found the root of all evil. He has shown us the way of salvation.

Buddha dispels the illusions of our minds and redeems us from the terrors of death.

Buddha, our Lord, brings comfort to the weary and sorrow-laden; he restores peace to those who are broken down under the burden of life. He gives courage to the weak when they would fain give up self-reliance and hope.

Ye that suffer from the tribulations of life, ye that have to struggle and endure, ye that yearn for a life of truth, rejoice at the glad tidings!

There is balm for the wounded, and there is bread for the hungry. There is water for the thirsty, and there is hope for the despairing. There is light for those in darkness, and there is inexhaustible blessing for the upright.

Heal your wounds, ye wounded, and eat your fill, ye hungry. Rest, ye weary, and ye who are thirsty quench your thirst. Look up to the light, ye that sit in darkness; be full of good cheer, ye that are forlorn.

Trust in truth, ye that love the truth, for the kingdom of righteousness is founded upon earth. The darkness of error is dispelled by the light of truth. We can see our way and make firm and certain steps.

Buddha, our Lord, has revealed the truth. The truth cures our diseases and redeems us from perdition; the truth strengthens us in life and in death; the truth alone can conquer the evils of error.

Rejoice at the glad tidings!

- Paul Carus,
Gospel of Buddha,
1905

CONTENTS

8 CONTENTS

INTRODUCTION

§ I

THE Dhammapada was accepted at the Council of Asoka in 240 B.C. as a collection of the sayings of Gautama ; yet it was not put into writing until some generations had passed, and probably contains accretions of later date.

However that may be, there is no doubt that it breathes the very spirit of the Teacher, and it has always been used in Buddhist lands as a handbook of " devotion " or meditation, in whose solemn precepts men hear the voice of Sakyamuni summoning them to the life of contemplation, of strenuous mind-culture. The world, it tells them, is without permanence or purpose, other than that of expiation ; the body is " a nest of disease " and the seat of " desire " ; the mind itself is subject to decay, and capricious, easily led away after false pursuits.

Yet here, in the mind of man, lies his hope of salvation : he may make it a strong tower of defence. Though the world is out of gear,

9

yet, like the Stoic, he may build within himself a kingdom and be at peace.

And so the call to "play the man" rings out with sturdy confidence. All men may attain, if they will, to happiness and serenity, for, with a modern Stoic, the Buddhist proclaims :

"I am the master of my fate ;
I am the captain of my soul."

Gautama then was no thoroughgoing pessimist ; that such a nature was pessimistic at all is due to the age in which he lived. It was the "sub-conscious mind" of his nation, and not his own brave spirit, that shut him in to the belief in a ceaseless flux of "becoming," a weary round of pain and retribution. For, by the sixth century B.C., India had passed from the sunny paganism of the Rig Veda into a more thoughtful and more gloomy phase of her religious development.

There were not wanting heroic spirits who offered a way of escape, urging men to plunge into asceticism or to court the mystic trance. These were the religious leaders of the day, at whose feet Gautama sat. Others, the great majority, were not ready for such heroic measures. They tried to square the gods, and to live unmolested, or to forget all in the pleasures of sense or the more subtle joys of the intellect.

To Gautama, all alike seemed "to follow

wandering fires." How degrading this thraldom
to immoral and capricious gods! How empty
and unsatisfying this mysticism when shorn of all
ethical content! Which is more to be pitied, the
grasping priest or the foolish worshipper? Which
more deluded, the worldling or the devotee ?

To all alike the Dhammapada has a message
of warning and encouragement : to the worldling
it holds out the promise of a truer wealth and
fame (75, 303) and a more blessed family life
(204-7, 302); to the warrior it offers a higher
" chivalry " (270) and a more heroic contest
(103, 104); to the philosopher a deeper wisdom
than much speaking (28, 100, 258); to the
mystic a purer and more lasting bliss (197-200); to
the devotee a more fruitful sacrifice (106-7); and
to the Brahmin a more ennobling service (§ xxvi)
and a more compelling authority (73, 74). It is,
in fact, possible largely to reconstruct the religious
life of Gautama's day from the stanzas of the
Dhammapada.

For all classes the Buddha has the same
message : the great reality is character; all
else are shadows not worth pursuing, for none
of them strengthens moral fibre, and all alike
are tainted with " desire."

Like Socrates, he saw in himself a physician of
the soul, and at times he resorted to surgery
to " stab the spirit broad awake," to call men
from superstition on the one hand and materialism

on the other. With Epictetus he would have
said, "A philosopher's school, my friends, is
a surgery, on leaving which you look to have
felt, not pleasure but pain."

Men needed above all things a moral tonic ;
there lies the secret at once of his stoicism and
his agnosticism ; luxury here, a barren mysticism
there—these were sapping men's strength, and
all the energy they could command was needed
in the fight for character. They must strive
and agonise to "cut out desire," to push their
way "against the stream," to cross life's stormy
"ocean" and reach the haven of peace. And
they must do it alone, not trusting to priest,
or sacrifice, or the help of Heaven.

For this insistence upon morality to the
exclusion of "religion" Gautama is often labelled
"atheist." Nothing could be more unfair :
agnostic he may have been or seemed to be ;
but his was no irreligious spirit : the man who
scoffs at the "other world" he condemns in
uncompromising terms, and Ethics so lofty as
this "Way of Virtue" never emanated from
any but a reverent spirit. It is one of the
puzzles of Psychology that so pure a soul ever
stopped short at Ethics ; yet we must remember
that he was a reformer, that reformers are apt
to be one-sided, and that during long and painful
years he had suffered at the hands of a false
"religiosity" ; the iron had entered into his soul.

" If Buddhists admit neither judge nor creator," says Professor de la Vallée Poussin, " at least they recognise a sovereign and infallible justice —a justice of wonderful insight and adaptability, however mechanically it acts. . . . In my opinion it is a calumny to accuse Buddhists of atheism : they have, at any rate, taken full cognisance of one of the aspects of the divine." *

Gautama believed above all things in a moral order, which, if it is inexorable, is also too righteous to yield to sacrificial bribes :

" Not in the sky, nor in mid-ocean, nor in mountain-cave, can one find sanctuary from his sin. . . . Often do men in terror seek sanctuary in mountains and in jungles, by sacred groves or trees : in them there is no safe sanctuary." (Dhammapada, 127, 188-9.)

So too the Psalmist cries, " Whither shall I flee from Thy presence ? If I ascend into heaven, Thou art there : if I go down to hell, Thou art there also."

Like the Hebrew prophet, too, he strikes a note of strenuous endeavour, of profound dissatisfaction with the actual, and of aspiration after the ideal : unlike the Hebrew and the Christian, he sees in the actual no promise of the ideal. His " way of salvation " is therefore monastic ; men are to leave the world if they would escape suffering and be truly happy : the layman may one day attain the far-off goal,

* Bouddhisme, p. 70.

but for him remains a long and weary pilgrimage, many revolutions of the wheel of existence.

It is to Bhikkhus then that these stanzas are in the main addressed. They are comments made by the Teacher to his disciples as occasion arose ; and to study them in a sympathetic spirit we of the West must for a time forget our impatience with "cloistered virtue." The saintly life in the world is no doubt a truer ideal than the saintly life out of it, yet saintliness of any type is not to be despised.

The Buddhist holds that in contemplative activity a man may best serve the world : is it not true that "we need reservoirs of every kind of excellence " ? We read in the Dhamma-pada of the fragrance of holy deeds which pervades the high heavens, and of the light that such a life may cast athwart a dark world. The "religious " is more to be envied than kings or even gods, and more fruitful.

> " Good is kingship of the earth ;
> Good attaining heavenly birth :
> World-conquest's good, but better far
> The fruits of true conversion are."
> (*Dhammapada*, 178.)

These fruits are "self-reverence, self-knowledge, self-control " (*cf.* 261) ; self-culture is in the end the truest benevolence, says the Buddhist, and the deepest wisdom. That "wisdom " of which we shall hear so much in the following pages, is "a certain over-mastering principle or power, that lays hold, primarily indeed, of the intellect, but through the intellect of the entire personality, moulding and disciplining the will and the emotions into absolute unison with itself, a principle from which courage, temperance, justice, and every other virtue inevitably flow." *

"A man is not wise by much speaking. . . . He is the wise man who is forgiving, kindly, and without fear." (*Dhammapada*, 258.)

For Gautama sees in ignorance not merely a calamity, but also a moral fault ; he agrees with the Darwinians in recognising in man the ape and the tiger, but adds, with Dr. Creighton, that "when the ape and the tiger go, there still remains the donkey, a far more formidable beast." †

Mōha, infatuation, and *Avijjā*, ignorance, are everywhere, and "Ignorance is the greatest of taints, more destructive than avarice and impurity." (*Ibid.*, 242, 243.)

He himself was the "enlightened," "the seer " who by insight had won emancipation, and he teaches that if men will only see things as they are, then they cannot but eschew evil and do good ; but the great multitude are

* Dr. J. Adam, *The Religious Teachers of Greece*, p. 329.
† Tibetan Buddhism illustrates these three cardinal vices by pictures of the cock (lust), the snake (anger), and the hog (stupidity).

fools and blind. To give them new ideals and
to lift the veil off their darkened hearts—this
was the work of Gautama, and in attempting it
he revealed a sturdy optimism and a magnetic
personality which went far to energise his ideal.
These qualities place him high amongst ethical
teachers.

§ II

And what shall we say of his system as religion ?
The student of these pages will find himself in
a moonlit world, beautiful yet cold :

"A common greyness silvers everything."

Here is no "sunset touch," no mystic hint of
Him "whose dwelling is the light of setting
suns "; our hearts are not stirred as we read
by any assurance of the reality of the Unseen.
Mysticism in short finds no entrance here—a
fact which makes the Dhammapada almost
unique amongst the great things of religious
literature. Instead we find "common sense"
supreme, mathematical, and a little cold, yet
confident of itself and of its firm grasp of all
the factors in life's equation. Instead of passion
and romance we shall find self-mastery and a
half-humorous sweet reasonableness. Everywhere Law is at work, and there is nothing
besides : no hint of whence law emanates, of
how it works, or why. These are questions alike

unprofitable and unanswerable. It is enough, the Buddha would say, that the world makes for righteousness, that sin is punished, and that goodness does not go unrewarded. " As you sow, so shall you reap." Happiness is the bloom upon virtue ; sorrow is the blight upon sin : and this is the ultimate motive to the strenuous life.

" Is such a world worth while ? " asks full-blooded Youth. "And is a calm like this enough ? " " The world," comes the serene answer, " is worth nothing at all : it has no reality and no purpose, save that of retribution : man's only happiness is to escape. The calm and peaceful frame of mind is the only happy one, the promise of a Rest hereafter, ineffable and placid ; to this man can and must attain."

K. J. S.

2

NOTE

An accurate and sympathetic knowledge of Buddhism and of the spirit of the Buddha is best got from such a book as the Dhammapada, which contains the concentrated essence of the religion. In view of widespread misinterpretation, a literal and accessible translation of this book, therefore, needs no apology. I have worked at the translation throughout with my friend Mr. Wagiswara, himself a Buddhist, and for many years a Bhikkhu ; that fact and the appearance of our translation in this series will vouch for sympathetic treatment in the rendering. It is notoriously difficult to find the exact English equivalents of Eastern terms, yet we trust that the spirit has been truly reproduced, and our version aims rather at accuracy than at elegance. Great thoughts are best " plain-set," and moreover it is impossible to reproduce the music of the old slokas of Indian poetry. We have referred frequently to Dr. Fausböll's Latin version, and occasionally to Professor Max Müller's edition in "The Sacred Books of the East." Only where the Sinhalese and Chinese commentaries are really illuminating have I referred to them in the notes, for which I am chiefly responsible.

K. J. S.

AND the Blessed One thought : "I have taught the truth which is excellent in the beginning, excellent in the middle, and excellent in the end ; it is glorious in its spirit and glorious in its letter. But simple as it is, the people cannot understand it. I must speak to them in their own language, I must adapt my thoughts to their thoughts. They are like unto children, and love to hear tales. Therefore, I will tell them stories to explain the glory of the dharma. If they cannot grasp the truth in the abstract arguments by which I have reached it, they may nevertheless come to under-stand it, if it is illustrated in parables."

- Paul Carus,
The Gospels of Buddha,
1905

THE BUDDHA'S "WAY OF VIRTUE"

§ I

THE TWIN TRUTHS

FOR the proper understanding of Buddhism these opening stanzas are all-important. One of the Buddha's key-thoughts was what modern psychologists call the "law of apperception": the value of things depends upon our attitude to them.

Part of Gautama's work of reform was a "transvaluation of values," a shifting of emphasis; and, like the Stoics, he taught the indifference of the things of sense. "Men are disturbed," said Epictetus, "not by things, but by the view they take of things."

·1. Mind it is which gives to things their quality, their foundation, and their being : whoso speaks or acts with impure mind, him sorrow dogs, as the wheel follows the steps of the draught-ox.

. 2. Mind it is which gives to things their quality,

their foundation, and their being: whoso speaks or acts with purified mind, him happiness accompanies as his faithful shadow.

3. "He has abused me, beaten me, worsted me, robbed me"; those who dwell upon such thoughts never lose their hate.

4. "He has abused me, beaten me, worsted me, robbed me"; those who dwell not upon such thoughts are freed of hate.

5. Never does hatred cease by hating; by not hating does it cease: this is the ancient law.

6. If some there are who know not by such hatred we are perishing, and some there are who know it, then by their knowledge strife is ended.

7. As the wind throws down a shaky tree, so Mara [Death] o'erwhelms him who is a seeker after vanity, uncontrolled, intemperate, slothful, and effeminate.

8. But whoso keeps his eyes from vanity, controlled and temperate, faithful and strenuous, Mara cannot overthrow, as the wind beating against a rocky crag.

9. Though an impure man don the pure yellow robe [of the Bhikkhu], himself unindued with temperance and truth, he is not worthy of the pure yellow robe.

10. He who has doffed his impurities, calm and clothed upon with temperance and truth, he wears the pure robe worthily.

11. Those who mistake the shadow for the

substance, and the substance for the shadow, never attain the reality, following wandering fires [lit. followers of a false pursuit].

12. But if a man knows the substance and the shadow as they are, he attains the reality, following the true trail.

13. As the rain pours into the ill-thatched house, so lust pours into the undisciplined mind.

14. As rain cannot enter the well-thatched house, so lust finds no entry into the disciplined mind.

15. Here and hereafter the sinner mourns : yea mourns and is in torment, knowing the vileness of his deeds.

16. Here and hereafter the good man is glad : yea is glad and rejoices, knowing that his deeds are pure.

17. Here and hereafter the sinner is in torment : tormented by the thought "I have sinned"; yea rather tormented when he goes to hell.

18. Here and hereafter the good man rejoices ; rejoices as he thinks "I have done well" : yea rather rejoices when he goes to a heaven.

19. If a man is a great preacher of the sacred text, but slothful and no doer of it, he is a hireling shepherd, who has no part in the flock.

20. If a man preaches but a little of the text and practises the teaching, putting away lust and hatred and infatuation ; if he is truly wise and detached and seeks nothing here or hereafter, his lot is with the holy ones.

§ II

ZEAL

ZEAL or earnestness (appamādo) plays an important part in Buddhist Ethics. The way is steep, therefore let the wayfarer play the man. Zeal may be displayed either in strenuous mind-culture or in deeds of piety—these are the equivalents of " Faith " and " Works " in the Buddhist system.

21. Zeal is the way to Nirvāna. Sloth is the day of death. The zealous die not : the slothful are as it were dead.

22. The wise who know the power of zeal delight in it, rejoicing in the lot of the noble.

23. These wise ones by meditation and reflection, by constant effort reach Nirvāna, highest freedom.

24. Great grows the glory of him who is zealous in meditation, whose actions are pure and deliberate, whose life is calm and righteous and full of vigour.

25. By strenuous effort, by self-control, by

temperance, let the wise man make for himself an island which the flood cannot overwhelm.

26. Fools in their folly give themselves to sloth : the wise man guards his vigour as his greatest possession.

27. Give not yourselves over to sloth, and to dalliance with delights : he who meditates with earnestness attains great joy.

28. When the wise one puts off sloth for zeal, ascending the high tower of wisdom he gazes sorrowless upon the sorrowing crowd below! Wise himself, he looks upon the fools as one upon a mountain-peak gazing upon the dwellers in the valley.

29. Zealous amidst the slothful, vigilant among the sleepers, go the prudent, as a racehorse outstrips a hack.

30. By zeal did Sakra reach supremacy among the gods. Men praise zeal ; but sloth is always blamed.

31. A Bhikkhu who delights in zeal, looking askance at sloth, moves onwards like a fire, burning the greater and the lesser bonds.

32. A Bhikkhu who delights in zeal, looking askance at sloth, cannot be brought low, but is near to Nirvāna.*

* Better, perhaps, " in the very presence of Nirvāna."

§ III

THE MIND

33. THIS trembling, wavering mind, so difficult to guard and to control—this the wise man makes straight as the fletcher straightens his shaft.

34. As quivers the fish when thrown upon the ground, far from his home in the waters, so the mind quivers as it leaves the realm of Death.

35. Good it is to tame the mind, so difficult to control, fickle, and capricious. Blessed is the tamed mind.

36. Let the wise man guard his mind, incomprehensible, subtle, and capricious though it is. Blessed is the guarded mind.

37. They will escape the fetters of Death who control that far-wandering, solitary, incorporeal cave-dweller, the mind.

38. In him who is unstable and ignorant of the law and capricious in his faith, wisdom is not perfected.

39. There is no fear in him, the vigilant one

whose mind is not befouled with lust, nor embittered with rage, who cares nought for merit or demerit.

40. Let him who knows that his body is brittle as a potsherd, make his mind strong as a fortress ; let him smite Mara with the sword of wisdom, and let him guard his conquest without dalliance.

41. Soon will this body lie upon the ground, deserted, and bereft of sense, like a log cast aside.

42. Badly does an enemy treat his enemy, a foeman his foe : worse is the havoc wrought by a misdirected mind.

43. Not mother and father, not kith and kin can so benefit a man as a mind attentive to the right.

§ IV

FLOWERS

44. Who shall conquer this world, and the realm of Death with its attendant gods ? Who shall sort the verses of the well-preached Law, as a clever weaver of garlands sorts flowers ?

45. My disciple shall conquer this world and Death with its attendant gods : it is he who shall sort the verses of the well-preached Law as a clever garland-maker sorts flowers.

46. Let him escape the eye of Mara, regarding his body as froth, knowing it as a mirage, plucking out the flowery shafts of Mara.

47. He who is busy culling pleasures, as one plucks flowers, Death seizes and hurries off, as a great flood bears away a sleeping village.

48. The Destroyer treads him underfoot as he is culling worldly pleasures, still unsated with lusts of the flesh.

49. As a bee taking honey from flowers, without hurt to bloom or scent, so let the sage seek his food from house to house.

50. Be not concerned with other men's evil

words or deeds or neglect of good : look rather to thine own sins and negligence [lit. "sins of commission and omission " : things done and undone].

51. As some bright flower—fair to look at, but lacking fragrance—so are fair words which bear no fruit in action.

52. As some bright flower, fragrant as it is fair, so are fair words whose fruit is seen in action.

53. As if from a pile of flowers one were to weave many a garland, so let mortals string together much merit.

54. No scent of flower is borne against the wind, though it were sandal, or incense or jasmine : but the fragrance of the holy is borne against the wind : the righteous pervade all space [with their fragrance].

55. More excellent than the scent of sandal and incense, of lily and jasmine, is the fragrance of good deeds.

56. A slight thing is this scent of incense and of sandal-wood, but the scent of the holy pervades the highest heaven.

57. Death finds not the path of the righteous and strenuous, who are set free by their perfect wisdom.

58, 59. As on some roadside dung-heap, a flower blooms fragrant and delightful, so amongst the refuse of blinded mortals shines forth in wisdom the follower of the true Buddha.

§ V

THE FOOL *

60. LONG is the night to the watcher, long is the league to the weary traveller : long is the chain of existence to fools who ignore the true Law.

61. If on a journey thou canst not find thy peer or one better than thyself, make the journey stoutly alone : there is no company with a fool.

62. " I have sons and wealth," thinks the fool with anxious care ; he is not even master of himself, much less of sons and wealth.

63. The fool who knows his folly is so far wise : but the fool who reckons himself wise is called a fool indeed.

64. Though for a lifetime the fool keeps company with the wise, yet does he not learn righteousness, as spoon gets no taste of soup.

65. If but for a moment the thoughtful keep company with the wise, straightway he learns righteousness, as tongue tastes soup.

66. Fools and dolts go their way, their own

* cf. Introduction, pp. 14, 15.

worst enemies : working evil which bears bitter fruit.

67. That is no good deed which brings remorse, whose reward one receives with tears and lamentation.

68. But that is the good deed which brings no remorse, whose reward the doer takes with joy and gladness.

69. Honey-sweet to the fool is his sin—until it ripens : then he comes to grief.

70. If once a month the fool sips his food from a blade of the sacred grass—his is no fraction of the Arahat's worth.

71. Evil does not straightway curdle like milk, but is rather like a smouldering fire which attends the fool and burns him.

72. When the fool's wisdom bears evil fruit it bursts asunder his happiness, and smashes his head.

73, 74. If one desire the praise of knaves, or leadership amongst the Bhikkhus, and lordship in the convents, and the reverence of the laity, thinking "Let layman and religious alike appreciate my deeds ; let them do my bidding and obey my prohibitions," if such be his fond imaginings, then will ambition and self-will wax great.

75. One is the road leading to gain, another is that leading to Nirvāna ; knowing this, let the Bhikkhu, the follower of Buddha, strive in solitude, not seeking the praise of men.

§ VI

THE WISE MAN

76. Look upon him who shows you your faults as a revealer of treasure : seek his company who checks and chides you, the sage who is wise in reproof : it fares well and not ill with him who seeks such company.

77. Let a man admonish, and advise, and keep others from strife ! So will he be dear to the righteous, and hated by the unrighteous.

78. Avoid bad friends, avoid the company of the evil : seek after noble friends and men of lofty character.

79. He who drinks in the law lives glad, for his mind is serene : in the law preached by the Noble the sage ever finds his joy.

80. Engineers control the water ; fletchers straighten the arrow ; carpenters fashion their wood. Sages control and fashion themselves.

81. As some massive rock stands unmoved by the storm-wind, so the wise stand unmoved by praise or blame.

82. As a deep lake, clear and undefiled, so are sages calmed by hearing the law.

83. Freely go the righteous; the holy ones do not whine and pine for lusts : unmoved by success or failure, the wise show no change of mood.

84. Desire not a son for thyself nor for another, nor riches nor a kingdom ; desire not thy gain by another's loss : so art thou righteous, wise, and good.

85. Few amongst men are they who reach the farther shore : the rest, a great multitude, stand only on the bank.

86. The righteous followers of the well-preached law, these are the mortals who reach the far shore. But hard is their journey through the realm of Death.

87, 88. Leaving the way of darkness, let the sage cleave to the way of light : let him leave home for the homeless life, that solitude so hard to love [Nirvāna]. Putting away lust and possessing nothing, let the sage cleanse himself from every evil thought.

89. They are serene in this world, whose mind is perfected in that clear thought which leads to Arahatship, whose delight is in renunciation, free from taints, and lustrous.

§ VII

90. No remorse is found in him whose journey is accomplished, whose sorrow ended, whose freedom complete, whose chains are all shaken off.

91. The mindful press on, casting no look behind to their home-life ; as swans deserting a pool they leave their dear home.

92. Some there are who have no treasure here, temperate ones whose goal is the freedom which comes of realising that life is empty and impermanent : their steps are hard to track as the flight of birds through the sky.

93. He whose taints are purged away, who is indifferent to food, whose goal is the freedom which comes of realising life's emptiness and transciency, is hard to track as the flight of birds in the sky.

94. Even the gods emulate him whose senses are quiet as horses well-tamed by the charioteer, who has renounced self-will, and put away all taints.

95. No more will he be born whose patience

is as the earth's, who is firm as a pillar and pious, pure as some unruffled lake.

96. Calm is the thought, calm the words and deeds of such a one, who has by wisdom attained true freedom and self-control.

97. Excellent is the man who is not credulous, who knows Nirvāna, who has cut all bonds, destroyed the germs of rebirth, cast off lust.

98. In the village or the jungle, on sea or land, wherever lives the Arahat, there is the place of delight.

99. Pleasant are the glades where the herd come not to disport themselves : there shall the Holy take their pleasure, who seek not after lust.

§ VIII

THE THOUSANDS

100. BETTER than a thousand empty words is one pregnant word, which brings the hearer peace.

101. Better than a thousand idle songs is a single song, which brings the hearer peace.

102. Better it is to chant one verse of the law, that brings the hearer peace, than to chant a hundred empty songs.

103. If one were to conquer a thousand thousand in the battle—he who conquers self is the greatest warrior.

104, 105. Self-conquest is better than other victories : neither god nor demi-god, neither Mara nor Brahma, can undo the victory of such a one, who is self-controlled and always calm.

106. If month by month throughout a hundred years one were to offer sacrifices costing thousands, and if for a moment another were to reverence the self-controlled—this is the better worship.

107. If one for a hundred years tended the

sacred fire in the glade, and another for a moment reverenced the self-controlled, this is the better worship.

108. Whatsoever sacrifice or offering a man makes for a full year in hope of benefits, all is not worth a quarter of that better offering— reverence to the upright.

109. In him who is trained in constant courtesy and reverence to the old, four qualities increase : length of days, beauty, gladness, and strength.

110. Better than a hundred years of impure and intemperate existence is a single day of moral, contemplative life.

111. Better is one day of wise and contemplative life than a thousand years of folly and intemperance.

112. Better one day of earnest energy than a hundred years of sloth and lassitude.

113. Better one day of insight into the fleeting nature of the things of sense, than a hundred years of blindness to this transiency.

114. Better one day of insight into the deathless state [Nirvāna], than a hundred years of blindness to this immortality.

115. Better one day of insight into the Supreme Law, than a hundred years of blindness to that Law.

§ IX

VICE

116. CLING to what is right : so will you keep the mind from wrong. Whoso is slack in well-doing comes to rejoice in evil.

117. If one offends, let him not repeat his offence ; let him not set his heart upon it. Sad is the piling up of sin.

118. If one does well, let him repeat his well-doing : let him set his heart upon it. Glad is the storing up of good.

119. The bad man sees good days, until his wrong-doing ripens ; then he beholds evil days.

120. Even a good man may see evil days till his well-doing comes to fruition ; then he beholds good days.

121. Think not lightly of evil "It will not come nigh me." Drop by drop the pitcher is filled : slowly yet surely the fool is saturated with evil.

122. Think not lightly of good "It will not come nigh me." Drop by drop the pitcher is

filled : slowly yet surely the good are filled with merit.

123. A trader whose pack is great and whose caravan is small shuns a dangerous road ; a man who loves his life shuns poison : so do thou shun evil.

124. He who has no wound can handle poison : the unwounded hand cannot absorb it. There is no evil to him that does no evil.

125. Whoso is offended by the inoffensive man, and whoso blames an innocent man, his evil returns upon him as fine dust thrown against the wind.

126. Some go to the womb ; some, evil-doers, to hell ; the good go to heaven ; the sinless to Nirvāna.

127. Not in the sky, nor in mid-ocean, nor in mountain-cave can one find sanctuary from his sins.

128. Not in the sky, not in mid-ocean, not in mountain-cave can one find release from the conquering might of death.

§ X

129. ALL fear the rod, all quake at death. Judge then by thyself, and forbear from slaughter, or from causing to slay.

130. To all is life dear. Judge then by thyself, and forbear to slay or to cause slaughter.

131. Whoso himself desires joy, yet hurts them who love joy, shall not obtain it hereafter.

132. Whoso himself desires joy and hurts not them who love it, shall hereafter attain to joy.

133. Speak not harshly to any one: else will men turn upon *you*. Sad are the words of strife: retribution will follow them.

134. Be silent as a broken gong: so wilt thou reach peace; for strife is not found in thee.

135. As the herdsman drives out his cows to the pasture, so Old Age and Death drive out the life of men.

136. Verily the fool sins and knows it not: by his own deeds is the fool tormented as by fire.

137. He who strikes those who strike not

and are innocent will come speedily to one of these ten states :

138. To cruel torment, loss, accident, severe illness, and madness he will come :

139. To visitation from the King, grievous slander, loss of kith and kin, and perishing of his wealth he will come:

140. Ravaging fire will destroy his houses, and after death the poor wretch will go to hell.

141. Not nakedness, nor matted hair, not dirt, nor fastings, not sleeping in sanctuaries, nor ashes, nor ascetic posture—none of these things purifies a man who is not free from doubt.

142. If even a fop fosters the serene mind, calm and controlled, pious and pure, and does no hurt to any living thing, he is the Brahmin he is the Samana, he is the Bhikkhu.

143. Is there in all the world a man so modest that he provokes no blame, as a noble steed never deserves the whip ? As a noble steed stung by the whip, be ye spirited and swift.

144. By faith, by righteousness, by manliness, by meditation, by just judgment, by theory and practice, by mindfulness, leave aside sorrow—no slight burden.

145. Engineers control the water, fletchers fashion their shafts, carpenters shape the wood : it is themselves that the pious fashion and control.

§ XI

OLD AGE

146. WHERE is the joy, what the pleasure, whilst all is in flames ?   Benighted, would ye not seek a torch ?

147. Look at this painted image, wounded and swollen, sickly and full of lust, in which there is no permanence ;

148. This wasted form is a nest of disease and very frail : it is full of putrid matter and perishes.   Death is the end of life.

149. What delight is there for him who sees these grey bones scattered like gourds in autumn ?

150. Here is a citadel of bones plastered with flesh and blood, and manned by old age and death, self-will and enmity.

151. As even the king's bright chariot grows old, so the body of man also comes to old age. But the law of the holy never ages : the holy teach it to the holy.

152. The simpleton ages like the ox: his weight increases, but not his wisdom.

153. Many births have I traversed seeking

the builder; in vain! Weary is the round of births.

154. Now art thou seen, O Builder. Nevermore shalt thou build the house! All thy beams are broken; cast down is thy cornerstone. My mind is set upon Nirvāna; it has attained the extinction of desire.

155. They who have not lived purely nor stored up riches in their youth, these ruefully ponder, as old herons by a lake without fish.

156. They who have not lived purely nor stored up riches in their youth, are as arrows that are shot in vain; they mourn for the past.

§ XII

SELF

157. IF a man love himself, let him diligently watch himself : the wise will keep vigil for one of the three watches of the night.

158. Keep first thyself aright ; then mayest thou advise others. So is the wise man unblameable.

159. If one so shapes his own life as he directs others, himself controlled, he will duly control others : self, they say, is hard to tame.

160. A man is his own helper : who else is there to help ? By self-control man is a rare help to himself.

161. The ill that is begun and has its growth and its being in self, bruises the foolish one, as the diamond pierces its own matrix.

162. As the creeper overpowers the tree, so he whose sin is great, works for himself the havoc his enemy would wish for him.

163. Ill is easy to do ; it is easy to do harm : hard indeed it is to do helpful and good deeds.

164. Whoso fondly repudiates the teaching

of the noble and virtuous Arahats, following false doctrine, is like the bamboo which bears fruit to its own destruction.

165. Thou art brought low by the evil thou hast done thyself : by the evil thou hast left undone art thou purified. Purity and impurity are things of man's inmost self ; no man can purify another.

166. Even for great benefit to another let no man imperil his own benefit. When he has realised what is for his own good, let him pursue that earnestly.

§ XIII

THE WORLD

167. LET no man foster evil habits ; let no man live in sloth : let none follow false doctrines, none prolong his sojourn in this world.

168. Up ! Idle not, but follow after good. The good man lives happy in this world and the next.

169. Follow after virtue, not after vice. The virtuous live happy in this world and the next.

170. The king of Death sees not him who regards the world as a bubble, a mirage.

171. Come then, think of the world as a painted chariot of the king—a morass where fools are sinking, where the wise take no pleasure.

172. He who in former days was slothful, and has put off sloth, lights up the world as the moon freed of the clouds.

173. He who covers his idle deeds with goodness lights up the world as the moon freed of clouds.

174. Blinded are the men of this world ; few there are who have eyes to see : few are the

birds which escape the fowler's net; few are they who go to heaven.

175. Through the sky fly the swans: Rishis too pass through the air. The wise leave the world altogether, deserting Mara and his hosts.

176. There is no wrong he would not do who breaks one precept, speaking lies and mocking at the life to come.

177. Misers go not to the realm of gods: therefore he is a fool who does not delight in liberality. The wise delighting in liberality come thereby with gladness to the other world.

178. Good is kingship of the earth; good is birth in heaven; good is universal empire; better still is the fruit of conversion.

§ XIV

THE BUDDHA

179. INTO his victory which is never reversed there enters no element of weakness : through what fault can you lead captive the faultless one, the Buddha whose sphere is Nirvāna ?

180. By what fault will you lead captive the faultless Buddha, whose sphere is Nirvāna ? In him are no clinging meshes of desire to lead him captive.

181. The gods themselves emulate the truly wise and mindful, who are busy in meditation and prudent, delighting in the peace of Nirvāna.

182. Arduous is human birth : arduous is mortal life : arduous is hearing of the Law : arduous the uprising of Buddhas.

183. " Eschew all evil ; cherish good ; cleanse your inmost thoughts "—this is the teaching of Buddhas.

184. " Patience and fortitude is the supreme asceticism : Nirvāna is above all," say the Buddhas. He is no recluse who harms others : nor is he who causes grief an ascetic [samana].

185. Hurt none by word or deed, be consistent in well-doing: be moderate in food, dwell in solitude, and give yourselves to meditation—this is the advice of Buddhas.

186. Not by a shower of gold is satisfaction of the senses found: "little pleasure, lasting pain," so thinks the sage.

187. The follower of the true Buddha finds no delight even in divine pleasures: but his joy is in the destruction of desire [tānhā].

188. Often do men in terror seek sanctuary in mountains or jungles, by sacred groves or trees;

189. In them is no safe sanctuary; in them is not the supreme sanctuary; in them is not that sanctuary whither a man may go and cast aside his cares.

190. But he who goes for sanctuary to the Buddha, the Dhamma, and the Sangha looks in his wisdom for the four noble truths:

191. "Sorrow, the arising of sorrow, the cessation of sorrow, and the noble eightfold path which leads to their cessation."

192. Here truly is the sure sanctuary; here is the supreme sanctuary: here is the sanctuary where a man may go and cast aside his care.

193. Hard to find is the Exalted One; he is not born in every place; happy dwells the household into which he, the wise one, is born:

194. A blessing is the arising of Buddhas, a blessing is the true preaching. Blessed is the

4

unity of the Sangha, blessed is the devotion of those who dwell in unity.

195, 196. Immeasurable is the merit of him who does reverence to those to whom reverence is due, Buddha and his disciples, men who have left behind them the trammels of evil, and crossed beyond the stream of sorrow and wailing, calmed and free of all fear.

§ XV

197. O Joy! We live in bliss; amongst men of hate, hating none. Let us indeed dwell among them without hatred.

198. O Joy! In bliss we dwell; healthy amidst the ailing. Let us indeed dwell amongst them in perfect health.

199. Yea in very bliss we dwell: free from care amidst the careworn. Let us indeed dwell amongst them without care.

200. In bliss we dwell possessing nothing: let us dwell feeding upon joy like the shining ones in their splendour.

201. The victor breeds enmity; the conquered sleeps in sorrow. Regardless of either victory or defeat the calm man dwells in peace.

202. There is no fire like lust; no luck so bad as hate. There is no sorrow like existence: no bliss greater than Nirvāna [rest].

203. Hunger is the greatest ill: existence is the greatest sorrow. Sure knowledge of this is Nirvāna, highest bliss.

204. Health is the greatest boon ; content is the greatest wealth ; a loyal friend is the truest kinsman ; Nirvāna is the Supreme Bliss.

205. Having tasted the joy of solitude and of serenity, a man is freed from sorrow and from sin, and tastes the nectar of piety.

206. Good is the vision of the Noble ; good is their company. He may be always happy who escapes the sight of fools.

207. He who consorts with fools knows lasting grief. Grievous is the company of fools, as that of enemies ; glad is the company of the wise, as that of kinsfolk.

208. Therefore do thou consort with the wise, the sage, the learned, the noble ones who shun not the yoke of duty : follow in the wake of such a one, the wise and prudent, as the moon follows the path of the stars.

§ XVI

209. He who gives himself to vanity and not to the truly profitable, shunning the true pursuit, and grasping at pleasure, will come to envy him who has sought the true profit.

210. Let no man cleave to what is pleasant or unpleasant : parting with the pleasant is pain, and painful is the presence of the unpleasant.

211. Take a liking to nothing ; loss of the prize is evil. There are no bonds for him who has neither likes nor dislikes.

212. From attachment comes grief, from attachment comes fear. He who is pure from attachment knows neither grief nor fear.

213. From affection come grief and fear. He who is without affection knows neither grief nor fear.

214. From pleasure come grief and fear. He who is freed from pleasure knows neither grief nor fear.

215. From lust come grief and fear. He who is freed from lust knows neither grief nor fear.

216. From desire come grief and fear. He who is free of desire knows neither grief nor fear.

217. The man of counsel and insight, of righteousness and truth, who minds his own affairs, him the crowd holds dear.

218. If a man's heart be set upon the Ineffable [Nirvāna], his mind brought to perfection, and every thought freed from lust, he is called the strong swimmer who forges his way against the stream.

219. When, after long voyaging afar, one returns in safety home, kinsfolk and friends receive him gladly ;

220. Even so his good deeds receive the good man, when he leaves this world for the next, as kinsfolk greet a dear traveller.

§ XVII

ANGER

221. Put away anger, eschew self-will, conquer every bond ; no suffering touches him who does not cling to phenomenal existence, but calls nothing his own.

222. Whoso controls his rising anger as a running chariot, him I call the charioteer : the others only hold the reins.

223. By calmness let a man overcome wrath ; let him overcome evil by good ; the miser let him subdue by liberality, and the liar by truth.

224. Speak the truth, be not angry, give of thy poverty to the suppliant : by these three virtues a man attains to the company of the gods.

225. The innocent, the sages, those whose action is controlled, these go to the eternal state where they know not sorrow [Nirvāna].

226. All taints pass away from them who are ever vigilant and active day and night, with faces set towards Nirvāna.

227. This is an ancient law, O Atula, not the law of a day : men blame the silent and they

blame the talker; even the man of few words they blame. No one in the world gets off unblamed.

228. There never was, nor will be, nor is there now to be found, one wholly blamed or wholly praised.

229, 230. But who is worthy to blame him whom the wise praise after daily scrutiny, who is himself wise and without blemish as a medal of purest gold? Even the gods seek to emulate such a one; even Brahma praises him.

231. Guard against evil deeds: control the body. Eschew evil deeds and do good.

232. Guard against evil words; control the tongue. Eschew evil words and speak good ones.

233. Guard against evil thoughts; control the mind. Eschew evil thoughts and think good ones.

234. The wise, controlled in act, in word, in thought, are well controlled indeed.

§ XVIII

SIN

235. Thou art withered as a sere leaf : Death's messengers await thee. Thou standest at the gate of death, and hast made no provision for the journey.

236. Make to thyself a refuge ; come, strive and be prudent : when thy impurities are purged, thou shalt come into the heavenly abode of the Noble.

237. Thy life is ended ; thou art come into the Presence of Death : there is no resting-place by the way, and thou hast no provision for the journey.

238. Make for thyself a refuge ; come, strive and play the sage ! Burn off thy taints, and thou shalt know birth and old age no more.

239. As a smith purifies silver in the fire, so bit by bit continually the sage burns away his impurities.

240. It is the iron's own rust that destroys it : it is the sinner's own acts that bring him to hell.

241. Disuse is the rust of mantras; laziness the rust of households; sloth is the rust of beauty; neglect is the watcher's ruin.

242. Impurity is the ruin of woman; and avarice the ruin of the giver: ill-deeds are the rust of this world and the next.

243. More corrosive than those is the rust of ignorance, the greatest of taints: put off this rust and be clean, O Bhikkhus.

244. Life is easy for the crafty and shameless, for the wanton, shrewd, and impure:

245. Hard it is for the modest, the lover of purity, the disinterested and simple and clean, the man of insight.

246, 247. The murderer, the liar, the thief, the adulterer, and the drunkard—these even in this world uproot themselves.

248. Know this, O man, evil is the undisciplined mind! See to it that greed and lawlessness bring not upon thee long suffering.

249. Men give according to faith or caprice. If a man fret because food and drink are given to another, he comes not day or night to serene meditation [i.e. Samādhi].

250. He in whom this [envious spirit] is destroyed and wholly uprooted, he truly day and night attains serene meditation.

251. There is no fire like lust, no ravenous beast like hatred, no snare like folly, no flood like desire.

252. To see another's fault is easy : to see one's own is hard. Men winnow the faults of others like chaff : their own they hide as a crafty gambler hides a losing throw.

253. The taints of this man are ever growing. He is far from the purification of taints [Arahatship], the censorious one who is ever blaming others.

254. There is no path through the sky : there is no "religious" apart from us. The world without delights in dalliance : the Blessed Ones are freed from this thrall.

255. There is no path through the sky ; there is no "religious" apart from us. Nothing in the phenomenal world is lasting ; but Buddhas endure immovable.

§ XIX

256, 257. Hasty judgment shows no man just. He is called just who discriminates between right and wrong, who judges others not hastily, but with righteous and calm judgment, a wise guardian of the law.

258. Neither is a man wise by much speaking : he is called wise who is forgiving, kindly, and fearless.

259. A man is not a pillar of the law for his much speaking : he who has heard only part of the law and keeps it indeed, he is a pillar of the law and does not slight it.

260. No man is made an " elder " by his grey locks : mere old age is called empty old age.

261. He is called " elder " in whom dwell truth and righteousness, harmlessness and self-control and self-mastery, who is without taint and wise.

262. Not by mere eloquence or comeliness is a man a " gentleman," who is lustful, a miser, and a knave.

263. But he in whom these faults are uprooted and done away, the wise and pure is called a gentleman.

264. Not by his shaven crown is one made a "religious" who is intemperate and dishonourable. How can he be a "religious" who is full of lust and greed ?

265. He who puts off entirely great sins and small faults—by such true religion is a man called "religious."

266. Not merely by the mendicant life is a man known as a mendicant : he is not a mendicant because he follows the law of the flesh ;

267. But because, being above good and evil, he leads a pure life and goes circumspectly.

268, 269. Not by silence [mona] is a man a sage [muni] if he be ignorant and foolish : he who holds as it were the balance, taking the good and rejecting the bad, he is the sage : he who is sage for both worlds, he is the true sage.

270. A man is no warrior who worries living things : by not worrying is a man called warrior.

271, 272. Not only by discipline and vows, not only by much learning, nor by meditation nor by solitude have I won to that peace which no worldling knows. Rest not content with these, O Bhikkhus, until you have reached the destruction of all taints.

§ XX

THE PATH

HAPPINESS is for Gautama, as for Aristotle, "the bloom upon virtue." The path which leads to the Supreme Bliss is the path of morality defined as the Noble Eightfold Path. If a man follow this, he is happy here and hereafter.

It consists of :

Right Views,
Right Aspirations,
Right Speech,
Right Action,
Right Livelihood,
Right Effort,
Right Mindfulness,
Right Contemplation.

This is described by Gautama as a Middle Path between the extreme of sensuality on the one hand and asceticism on the other; or between superstitious credulity and sceptical materialism. It is a truly noble ideal: yet one must never forget that "Righteousness" throughout is Buddhistically defined: *e.g.* "Right Views" means a correct grasp of the Buddhist teaching that all is transient, all is sorrowful, all is unreal. Again, "Right Contemplation" is the practice of Samādhi, concentration of the mind upon Buddhist ideas, such as the above. The highest "Livelihood," again, is to live upon the alms of the faithful.

273. Best of paths is the Eightfold; the four truths are the best of truths : purity is the best state ; best of men is the seer.

274. This is the way; there is none other that leads to the seeing of Purity [Nirvāna.] Do you follow this path : that is to befool Mara.

275. Travelling by this way you'll end your grief : it is the way I preached when I learnt to throw off my bonds.

276. 'Tis you who must strive : the Blessed Ones are only preachers. They who strive and meditate are freed from Mara's bonds.

277. "All is passing " : when one sees and realises this, he sits loose to this world of sorrow : this is the way of purity.

278. "All is sorrow " : when one sees and realises this, he sits loose to this world of sorrow : this is the way of purity.

279. "All is unreal " : when one sees and realises this, he sits loose to this world of sorrow : this is the way of purity.

280. He who fails to strive when 'tis time to strive, young and strong though he be, slothful and enmeshed in lust, the sluggard, never finds the path to wisdom.

281. Whoso guards his tongue and controls his mind and does nothing wrong : keeping clear these three paths, he will achieve the way shown by the wise.

282. From meditation springs wisdom ; from neglect of it the loss of wisdom. Knowing this path of progress and decline, choose the way that leads to growth of wisdom.

283. Cut down the jungle (I do not mean with an axe!). For from the jungle of lust springs fear, and if you cut it down, you will be disentangled, O Bhikkhus !

284. Whilst the entanglement of a man with a woman is not utterly cut away, he is in bondage, running to her as a sucking calf to the cow.

285. Pluck out the bond of self as one pulls up an autumn lotus. Forge thy way along the path of safety, Nirvāna, shown by the Blessed.

286. "Here will I pass the wet season ; here the winter and summer," thinks the fool, unmindful of what may befall.

287. Then comes Death and sweeps him away infatuated with children and cattle, and entangled with this world's goods, as a flood carries off a sleeping village.

288. There is no safety in sons, or in father,

or in kinsfolk when Death overshadows thee :
amongst thine own kith and kin is no refuge :
289. Knowing this clearly, the wise and
righteous man straightway clears the road that
leads to Nirvāna.

5

§ XXI

290. IF at the cost of a little joy one sees great joy, he who is wise will look to the greater and leave the less.

291. Whoso seeks his own pleasure by another's pain, is entangled in hate and cannot get free.

292. Duty neglected; evil done: the taints of the proud and slothful wax ever more and more.

293. But those who are ever pondering the nature of the body, who run not after evil, who are constant in duty—in these, the vigilant and wise, taints come utterly to an end.

294. Having destroyed Mother and Father and two noble Kings, with the whole Kingdom and its Vizier, innocent goes the Brahmin!

295. Innocent goes the Brahmin having destroyed Mother and Father and two Brahmin Kings, and the five Roads and their fierce guardians.

296. The followers of Gautama are ever vigilant; their thought day and night is set upon Buddha.

297-301. The followers of Gautama are ever vigilant ; day and night is their thought set upon the Dhamma, the Sangha, the body, compassion [not harming], mind-culture.

302. Hard it is to leave home as a recluse ! hard also to live at home as a householder ; hard is the community life ; the lot of the wanderer in the world is also hard.

303. The faithful, upright man is endowed with [the true] fame and wealth, and is honoured wherever he goes.

304. Far off are seen the Holy Ones, like the Himālayas : the unholy pass unseen as arrows shot in the darkness.

305. Alone when eating, alone when sleeping, alone when walking, let a man strongly control himself and take his pleasure in the forest glade.

§ XXII

HELL

306. THE liar goes to hell, and the villain who denies his crime ; these mean ones are alike in the world beyond.

307. Though clad in yellow robe, the man of many sins who is uncontrolled is born in hell : the sinner is punished by his sin.

308. Better to swallow a ball of red-hot iron than to live uncontrolled upon the bounty of the faithful.

309. Four evil consequences follow the sluggard and the adulterer : retribution, broken slumber, an evil name, and in the end hell.

310. That way lie retribution and an evil character, the short-lived joy of trembling sinners, and a heavy penalty from the ruler. Therefore run not after thy neighbour's wife.

311. As pampas-grass clumsily handled cuts the hand, so is the community life ; abused, it brings a man to hell.

312. All duties carelessly performed ; all vows

slightingly observed; the recluse life that is open to suspicion—these bear no great fruit.

313. If a duty is to be done, do it with thy might: a careless recluse scatters contagion broadcast.

314. Better leave undone a bad deed; one day the doer will lament: good it is to do the good deed which brings no remorse.

315. As a fortress guarded within and without, so guard thyself. Leave no loophole for attack! They who fail at their post mourn here, and hereafter go to hell.

316. Some are ashamed at what is not shameful, and blush not at deeds of shame: these perverse ones go to hell.

317. They who see fear where there is no fear, and tremble not at fearful things: these perverse ones go to hell.

318. They who think evil where there is no evil, and make light of grievous sin: these perverse ones go to hell.

319. But whoso calls sin sin, and innocence innocence: these right-minded ones go to happiness.

§ XXIII

THE elephant is the symbol in Buddhism of endurance and solitary strength.

320. I will endure abuse as the elephant endures the arrow in the battle : evil is the crowd.

321. Men lead the tamed elephant into battle ; upon his back the king rides : he who is tamed and endures abuse patiently is praised of men.

322. Noble are the tamed mules ; noble the blood-horses of Sindh, and the great elephants of war : better is he who has tamed himself.

323. Not by bridling them will one journey to the unknown shore [Nirvāna], but by bridling himself.

324. Dhānapālako, the great elephant, is hard to control in the time of rut : he will not taste his food in captivity, but longs after the elephant-grove.

325. If one becomes a sluggard or a glutton, rolling over in gross sleep like a stall-fed hog,

again and again does he come to the womb, the foolish one !

326. This mind of mine would wander in days of old whither desire and lust and caprice led it : now will I control it as a mahout controls the elephant in rut.

327. Be ye zealous : guard your thoughts. As an elephant sunk in the mud extricate yourselves from the clutches of evil.

328. If you can find a dutiful friend to go with you, a righteous and prudent man not caring for hardships, go with him deliberately.

329. If you cannot find such a one, travel alone as a king leaving a conquered realm, or as the elephant in the jungle.

330. It is better to be alone ; there is no companionship with a fool : travel alone and sin not, forgetting care as the elephant in the jungle.

331. Good are companions in time of need ; contentment with thy lot is good ; at the hour of death, merit is a good friend, and good is the leaving of all sorrow.

332. Good is reverence for mother and father : good, too, reverence for recluses and sages.

333. Good is lifelong righteousness ; and rooted faith is good : good is the getting of wisdom, and good the avoiding of sin.

§ XXIV

DESIRE

Tanhā (desire) is defined as the hankering after pleasure, or existence, or success (or all three). (Mahavagga xvi. 20.) It is the germ from which springs all human misery: birth, old age, and suffering. To be rid of Tanhā is to be free of pain, to pass into the Beyond, the painless dream-world of Nirvāna.

334. As the "maluwa" creeper, so spreads the desire of the sluggard. From birth to birth he leaps like a monkey seeking fruit.

335. Whoso is subdued by this sordid clinging desire, his sorrows wax more and more, like "birana" grass after rain.

336. But *his* sorrows drop off like water from the lotus leaf, who subdues this sordid, powerful desire.

337. I give you this good counsel, all ye who are gathered here: cut out desire as one digs up the grass to find the fragrant root. Let ·

not Mara break you again and again as the river breaks the rushes.

338. A tree, though it be cut down, yet springs up again, if its roots are safe and firm : thus sorrow, if it be not uprooted, springs repeatedly to birth.

339. If man's desires flow unchecked, the waves of his lust and craving bear him off—misguided one !

340. Everywhere flow the streams ; everywhere the creeper sprouts and takes hold. If thou seest this creeper growing, be wise ! pluck it out by the roots.

341. Men hug delights ; they foster some pet sin, hankering after which they suffer birth and old age.

342. Dogged by lust, men double like a hunted hare. Fast bound in its fetters, they go through long ages to misery.

343. Dogged by lust, they double like a hunted hare. Throw off thy lust, O Bhikkhu, if thou wouldst be free.

344. Whoso has left the tangle of home-life for the solitude of the jungle, and goes back to it, regard him thus : "Lo, one who was freed, and ran back to his chains."

345. Iron and wood and hemp—these sages call not heavy bonds, but rather love of bejewelled women, and the care for children and wives.

346. This is a heavy bond indeed : light

though it seem, it drags men down, and is not easily cut off. Yet some there are who cut even this asunder, and leave behind them pleasure and lust, with no backward glance.

347. Some again there are who fall into the meshes of their own lust as the spider falling into her own net : even this the wise cut through, leaving sorrow behind, with no backward glance.

348. Lay aside past, future, and present, escaping the world : wholly freed in mind, thou shalt not again return to birth and old age.

349. Desire waxes great in him who is oppressed by wandering thoughts, fired with lust and seeking after pleasure. So doth he make his fetters strong.

350. Whoso delights in calming his thoughts and looks askance at the things of sense, will thus come to an end, and cut the bonds of Mara.

351. This will be his last body, who has reached the goal, who is fearless, detached, and un-blameable : who has pulled out the rivets of existence.

352. He who is detached and not grasping, a clever student of the law and its meaning, knowing the words and their order, he is called the enlightened ; this is his last birth.

353. "All conquering and all knowing am I, detached, untainted, untrammelled, wholly freed by destruction of desire. Whom shall I call Teacher ? Myself found the way."

354. The gift of the Law surpasses every gift ; the savour of the Law surpasses every savour ; the pleasure of the Law surpasses every pleasure. The destruction of desire conquers all sorrow.

355. Wealth kills the fool if he look not to the Beyond : for greed of wealth fools kill each other.

356. Weeds are the bane of fields, and lust the bane of the crowd. Therefore a gift given where there is no lust bears much fruit.

357-9. Weeds are the bane of fields; wrath, infatuation, and avarice are the bane of the crowd. A gift given where there is neither wrath, nor infatuation, nor avarice bears much fruit.

§ XXV

THE BHIKKHU

360. GOOD is restraint of eye and ear : of smell and taste.

361. Good is restraint of action and of speech ; restraint of mind and of every sense is good. The Bhikkhu restrained in all things casts aside every care.

362. Best amongst the temperate is he who is temperate in hand and foot and tongue : the man of inward joy and calm, him I call Bhikkhu.

363. The Bhikkhu who is temperate and moderate in speech, not puffed up, but a wise preacher and interpreter—sweet are his words !

364. He who abides in the law and takes his pleasure therein, revolving it in his mind and pondering it, he is a Bhikkhu who falls not away from the Law.

365. Let him neither make much of his own gain, nor envy that of others : the Bhikkhu who envies others attains not the true meditation.

366. Even the gods praise that Bhikkhu whose

own gain is slight, yet who covets not the gain of other men, but lives pure and strenuous.

367. He who clings not to self-hood and to existence, but mourns at the vanity of this fleeting world, he is called Bhikkhu.

368. The Bhikkhu who lives kindly and trusts in Buddha's Teaching he approaches Nirvāna, the calm and blissful end of rebirth.

369. Bale out the ship, O Bhikkhu, then will it go lightly ; cut the thongs of lust and hate ; so wilt thou come to Nirvāna.

370. Cut the five bonds, leave other five, and take in their place five more : he who has got beyond the five evil states is said to have crossed the flood.

371. Keep vigil, O Bhikkhu, be not slothful, let not your mind dally with delights : suffer not the pangs of hell, and wail not as the flames devour you, " O day of woe " !

372. There is no meditation apart from wisdom ; there is no wisdom apart from meditation. Those in whom wisdom and meditation meet are not far from Nirvāna.

373. Divine pleasure is his who enters into solitude, the Bhikkhu who is calmed and sees the law with the seeing eye :

374. Whenever he ponders the beginning and the end of the elements of being, he finds joy and bliss ; nectar it is to those who know.

375. This is the beginning in my teaching for

a wise Bhikkhu ; self-mastery, contentment, and control by the precepts : to cultivate those who are noble, righteous, and zealous friends ;

376. To be hospitable and courteous, this is to be glad and to make an end of sorrow.

377. As jasmine sheds its withered blossoms so, O Bhikkhus, do you put away lust and hatred.

378. He who is controlled in act, in speech, in thought, and altogether calmed, having purged away worldliness, that Bhikkhu is called calm.

379. Come, rouse thyself ! Examine thine own heart. The Bhikkhu who is thus self-guarded and mindful will live in happiness.

380. Each man is his own helper, each his own host ; therefore curb thyself as the merchant curbs a spirited horse.

381. The glad Bhikkhu who puts his trust in Buddha's Preaching goes to Nirvāna, calm and blissful end of rebirth.

382. Let the young Bhikkhu apply himself to Buddha's Preaching : so will he light up the world as the moon escaped from the clouds.

§ XXVI

383. PLAY the man and stem the flood of passion !
Cast off your lusts, O Brahmin ; having known
the ending of the perishable, thou knowest the
imperishable, O Brahmin.

384. When the Brahmin has travelled the
twofold path of meditation, then indeed his
chains fall off him, for he knows the truth.

385. Him I call the Brahmin whom desire
assails not from within nor from without, in
whom is no fear, he is indeed free.

386. Him I call Brahmin who is meditative,
clean of heart, solitary, who has done his duty
and got rid of taints, who has reached the goal
of effort.

387. The sun shines by day, the moon lights
up the night ; radiant is the soldier in his panoply,
radiant the Brahmin in his meditation ; but
the Buddha in his brightness is radiant day
and night.

388. By Brahmin   mean one who has put

away evil ; for his serenity is a man called
Samano ; for excluding his own sin is a man
called recluse.

389. Do no evil to a Brahmin ; let not the
Brahmin return evil for evil. Woe to him who
kills a Brahmin ; yea, rather, woe to that Brahmin
who loses his temper !

390. It is no slight benefit to a Brahmin when
he learns to hold his impulses in check ; from
whatever motive evil temper is controlled, by
that control grief is truly soothed.

391. By whomsoever no evil is done in deed,
or word, or thought, him I call a Brahmin who
is guarded in these three.

392. As the Brahmin honours the burnt-
sacrifice, so do thou honour him, from whomsoever is learnt the law of the true Buddha.

393. Not by matted locks, nor by lineage,
nor by caste is one a Brahmin ; he is the
Brahmin in whom are truth and righteousness
and purity.

394. What boots your tangled hair, O fool,
what avails your garment of skins ? You have
adorned the outer parts, within you are full of
uncleanness.

395. A man clothed in cast-off rags, lean,
with knotted veins, meditating alone in the
forest, him I call a Brahmin.

396. Not him do I call Brahmin who is merely
born of a Brahmin mother ; men may give him

salutation as a Brahmin, though he be not detached from the world : but him I call a Brahmin who has attachment to nothing.

397. Him I call a Brahmin who has cut the bonds, who does not thirst for pleasures, who has left behind the hindrances.

398. Whoso has cut the cable, and the rope and the chain with all its links, and has pushed aside the bolt, this wise one I call a Brahmin.

399. Whoever bears patiently abuse and injury and imprisonment, whose bodyguard is fortitude, he is the Brahmin.

400. He is the Brahmin who does not give way to anger, who is careful of religious duties, who is upright, pure, and controlled, who has reached his last birth.

401. He who clings not to pleasures as water clings not to the lotus leaf, nor mustard-seed to the needle-point, him I call Brahmin.

402. He is the Brahmin who in this very world knows the end of sorrow, who has laid the burden aside and is free.

403. Whoso is wise with deep wisdom, seeing the right way and the wrong, and has reached the goal, him I call Brahmin.

404. He is the Brahmin who is not entangled either with householders or with recluses, who has no home and few wants.

405. He who lays down the rod, who neither

6

kills, nor causes the death of creatures, moving or fixed, he is the Brahmin.

406. Not opposing those who oppose, calm amidst the fighters, not grasping amidst men who grasp, he is the Brahmin.

407. He is the Brahmin from whom anger, and hatred, and pride, and slander have dropped away, as the mustard-seed from the needle-point.

408. If one were to preach gentle, and instructive, and truthful words by which no man is offended, he is the Brahmin.

409. Whoso takes nothing small or great, good or bad, unless it be given him, he is the Brahmin.

410. In whom are found no longings, who is free and detached from this world and the next, he is the Brahmin.

411. Him I call a Brahmin in whom lust is not found, who has cast off doubt, who knows the path that leads to Nirvāna [the deathless state] and reaches it.

412. Who in this life has passed from the grip of either merit or demerit, free of sorrow, cleansed and purified, him I call Brahmin.

413. Who is clear as the moon, pure, and limpid, and serene, who has quenched his thirst for life ;

414. Who has passed through this impassable quagmire of rebirth, and infatuation, has waded

through it and got beyond it, who is meditative and supplies no fuel to the fires of lust and doubt, him I call a Brahmin.

415. Who in this life, deserting his lusts, goes from home into solitude, and has quenched lust, and with it the desire to be reborn ;

416. Who in this life deserts craving, and goes from home into solitude, who has quenched craving, and with it the desire to be reborn, him I call Brahmin.

417. Who has left behind him human pleasures and passed beyond heavenly ones, and is freed from all entanglement of delight ;

418. Who has left aside both gusto and disgust, who is cooled and has in him no spark of rebirth, victor'in all worlds, and hero, him I call Brahmin.

419. He is the Brahmin who fully knows the perishing of living things and their uprising, who is detached and happy and wise.

420. He is the Brahmin whose way is not known to gods, nor heavenly minstrels, nor immortals ; the Arahat pure of all taint, him I call the Brahmin.

421. Whoso has nothing left, of past or future or present states, who is poor and grasps at nothing, him I call Brahmin.

422. The Leader Supreme, the heroic, the great Rishi, the Victor without lust and purified, the Buddha, he is the Brahmin.

423. He is the Brahmin indeed who knows his former lives, and who knows heaven and hell, who has reached the end of births, the sage whose knowledge is perfect, and who is perfect vith all perfection.

THE END

OF

THE DHAMMAPADA

NOTES

1, 2. THESE stanzas contain two ideas which are of the very warp and woof of Buddhism :

    (*a*) The view depends upon the point of view ;

    (*b*) Thought is potent in influencing man's destiny.

The Chinese Commentary illustrates both these ideas: Two merchants listened to the Buddha's preaching ; one was delighted, the other angry : men hear what they are prepared to hear. Soon after one was killed, the other became King : so potent is thought !

8. *Cf.* Luke vi, 48.

9, 10. The Buddha often used a play upon words to arrest men's attention and help their memory. The Pali of these stanzas contains a pun of this kind, which cannot be imitated in English : *Kāsāvam* means either the yellow robe of the mendicant, or impurity, stain, sin.

11, 12. The work of Gautama as a preacher lay largely in this directing of men's efforts : the great reality is character ; this and this alone is man's business upon earth.

All else are " shadows " not worth pursuing. *Cf.* St. John's words: " Little children, flee idols " (*i.e.* " shadows "), 1 John v, 21. So St. Paul speaks of covetousness as " idolatry "—the pursuit of the ' great " shadow," Mammon (Col. iii, 5).

When the Buddhist puts on the yellow robe, he symbolises his belief that " virtue is the truest wealth ": the gold of character is alone worth striving after. (*Cf.* Dhammapada, 75 and note.) On the day of his ordination (upasampadā) the candidate adorns himself with all the jewellery he can obtain, and doffs it only to don the yellow robe.

15-18. *Here* and *Hereafter :* *i.e.* in this birth and the next. Man may be reborn upon earth, or in one of the hells or in one of the heavens. A demon who does well may become a man or a god: a god who lives unworthily may become a man or a demon.

Tormented when he goes to hell. The Buddhist Temples are full of frescoes of these torments : men who have killed animals are being slowly devoured by them ; other sinners are being forced by demon torturers to climb spiky trees, or burnt in fires most realistically drawn, or made to swallow balls of red-hot iron ; low-caste men who have offended the high castes are being crushed by great rocks !

The Buddha's own discourses contain minute detail of such torments. It is not clear whether he was using an *argumentum ad hominem*, or really believed in a hereafter of physical torment. In any case his moral code has been strangely perverted in modern Buddhism.

18. The reward for virtue is twofold—the approval of conscience and a good rebirth.

19. *Cf.* Matt. xxiii, 2 ; John x, 12.

20. *The holy ones :* Arahats, those who have attained. The sentence means : " he is on his way to Nirvāna."

21. *Amatapadam* : lit. " The endless or deathless state" (Fausböll). Nirvāna is defined by many such phrases in the Dhammapada—sometimes negative, as here ; sometimes positive, as in 23—" highest freedom." Whatever the Supreme Bliss be, it is unlike all human experience save that of the Arahat.

Rhys Davids translates " ambrosia, or nectar."

As it were dead : i.e. spiritually or morally dead. *Cf.* " Let the dead bury their dead," Matt. viii, 22, and " The life of the fool is worse than death," Ecclus. xxii, 11.

22. *The lot of the Noble.* The word " Aryo " meant in Gautama's day Nobleman, or Aryan. He defined the nobleman anew, making nobility consist not in birth, but in conduct. Then he developed the meaning till it stood for Arahats— the experts in his system, those who have attained.

23. *Meditation :* jhānam—that ecstatic contemplation in which the mind, rapt from the sounds and sights of the

ordinary world, concentrates itself upon some single object or idea; this leads to serenity and a unique bliss, anticipation of Nirvāna.

Highest freedom. Nirvāna is complete freedom from : (1) The body and suffering; (2) Desire and other taints.

25. *An island : i.e.* Nirvāna.

Self-control, temperance. Buddhism makes much of the " cardinal virtues."

26. The Buddhist motto may be said to be " Strive without ceasing."

27. The joy which is born of meditation plays a great part in Buddhist psychology and ethics. (*Cf.* Rhys Davids' *Early Buddhism*, pp. 62-5.)

28. Contrast this somewhat Epicurean attitude with St. Paul's exhortation " Rejoice with them that do rejoice, and weep with them that weep " (Rom. xii, 15).

The Buddhist position is in reality midway between the Epicurean and the Christian; it is stoical: the attitude to be assumed towards the " crowd " is either *mettam*, benevolence if (one's own salvation being certain) one can help them: or it is *upekha*, detachment. " What can't be cured must be endured." *Muditā*, sympathy, and *Karunā*, pity, are also duties, but it is no use wasting these upon the blinded and foolish crowd. (*Cf.* 61, 64.)

30. *Sakra : i.e.* Indra, a high god of Hinduism whom Buddhism has relegated to the rank of an archangel, ruling the Tavatimsa heaven. He is said to have been a young Brahmin who for his zeal in doing good was reborn as Sakra. His human name was Magha. He is regarded by Buddhists as a kind of recording angel. (Childers.)

31. *Bhikkhu.* The " religious " of Buddhism is neither " priest " nor " monk " in the strict sense, for he offers no sacrifice, and he lives not alone, but either with one or two others, or with the " community." The word " bhikkhu " means " mendicant."

The greater and the lesser bonds : all those "trammels" which bind him to the phenomenal world; all that affects his senses,

33. In his doctrine of the mind, Gautama was no pessimist ; it is by nature fickle and difficult to control : yet nurture can make it stable and obedient. (*Cf.* especially 40, where Gautama's optimistic attitude to the mind is thrown into strong relief by his pessimistic attitude to the body ; if the body be brittle and of slight value, yet the mind may be made strong and precious.) His pessimistic attitude to the body is partly assumed with intent " to wean men from it," and this view is borne out by the genial attitude he takes towards asceticism : once a man has learnt to sit loose to the things of sense he is free to enjoy them. Gautama laid himself open to the name of worldling, and the immediate cause of his death was his courteous acceptance of the rich meal prepared for him by Cunda the smith.

34. The simile is obscure : it is apparently only intended to make one point clear—the palpitating effort needed to escape Mara.

39. *Merit.* The desire for merit is almost universal in Buddhist lands ; yet Buddha teaches that man should act with his eye fixed not upon " merit," but upon Nirvāna. (But *cf.* 53.) By " merit " is meant the credit balance in the bank of character—procuring rebirth to a happy life on earth, or in a heaven.

46. *The flowery shafts of Mara :* the insidious advances of the King of Death. *Cf.* Ps. v, 9 : " They flatter with their tongue."

49. The mendicant is to take what is given him by the faithful, doing them no harm, and taking nothing but what they freely give.

51. *Cf.* Matt. xxiii, 3 : " They say and do not."

54. Natural law is not universally valid in the spiritual world !

56. Certain "*rishis*," having neglected cleanliness in their pursuit of holiness, were ashamed to come into the presence of the gods : " Never fear," said the gods, " our nostrils are filled with the fragrance of your good deeds."

Cf. our phrases : " The odour of sanctity " ; " The beauty of holiness."

61. According to Buddhism neither will profit by such companionship. (*Cf.* 64.)

64. *Cf.* Ecclus. xxii, 7 : " He that teacheth a fool is as one that glueth a potsherd together."

70. *i.e.* extreme asceticism and religious observance are not worth a tithe of goodness.

73-4. Ambition and self-will are the besetting faults of the Brahmin.

75. *Cf.* " Ye cannot serve God and Mammon."

76. The wise will value a candid friend.

79. A better draught than the soma juice, which led to ecstasy !

89. *That leads to Arahatship.* Sambōdhi (Arahatship) has seven component parts, which may be taken to represent the Buddhist ideal of character : mindfulness, wisdom, energy, joyousness, serenity, concentrated meditation, and equanimity.

Whose delight is in renunciation. Cf. Bhagavad-Gita xii :
     " Near to renunciation—very near—
     Dwelleth eternal Peace."

92, 93. *Whose goal is the freedom . . .* A definition of Nirvāna. The Commentator explains the simile as expressing the mysterious freedom of Arahats in the spiritual sphere. (*Cf.* " The wind bloweth where it listeth, and thou hearest the sound of it, but canst not tell whence it cometh and whither it goeth : *So is every one that is born of the Spirit.*" —John iii, 8.)

94. *Even the gods.* The true Buddhist is above all gods !

Charioteer. Cf. Plato's famous simile of the Charioteer Reason and the two horses of Sensibility and Spirit : one rebellious, the other docile. *Cf.* also " The spirit is willing, but the flesh is weak."

95. *Whose patience is as the earth's :* the earth does not shrink or protest whatever is laid upon it.

97. This is one of those curious enigmas or puzzles which

occur in the Buddha's teaching. It can be translated in a sense opposed to that here given: viz. "*Best of men is the faithless, the ungrateful, the rebel, who has lost his chance of salvation, who has given up all hope.*" It was spoken by Gautama to some thirty recluses who accused Sāriputto of these faults, because he told his master not to preach to him, but to them, "I already know the truth by experience; these others need it on authority: therefore preach to them." Buddha's words express with great skill the two ways in which he and the recluses looked upon his disciple's sturdy confidence. It is of course quite impossible in an analytic language like English to reproduce the puns.

100. *Cf.* St. Paul: "I had rather speak five words with my understanding, that I might instruct others also, than ten thousand words in a tongue." (1 Cor. xiv, 19.)

103-5. *Cf.* Prov. xvi, 32: "He that is slow to anger is better than the mighty: and he that ruleth his spirit han he that taketh a city."

104, 105. Buddhist ethics make much of the truth that external forces cannot harm the true man: man cannot be hurt except by himself. (*Cf.* 124.)

106. *Cf.* 1 Sam. xv, 22: "To obey is better than sacrifice."

109. *Cf.* Manu, II, 121: and Asoka's Rock Edict, II: "Father and mother must be hearkened to . . . this leads to length of days." *Cf.* also the fifth commandment of the Decalogue: "Honour thy father and thy mother that thy days may be long in the land."

110, 111. *Cf.* the Psalmist: "One day in Thy courts is better than a thousand."

125. Gautama again and again insists that natural law holds good in the spiritual world, though there are exceptions. (*Cf.* 54.)

126. *Go to the womb:* i.e. are born upon earth.

127-8. *Cf.* Introduction, p. 13.

129-32. *Cf.* Luke vi, 31: The Golden Rule.

141. *Doubt:* one of the deadly sins in Buddhism. The Buddha claimed omniscience, and though he did not dis-

courage investigation and inquiry, from the great mass of men, who are ignorant and foolish, he demanded the plunge of faith.

Matted hair, etc. The Sumāgadhā-avadāna relates that Sumāgadhā, seeing the naked and unkempt ascetics of Brahminism, exclaimed: " O Mother, if these are saints, what must sinners be like ? " (*Cf.* Max Müller's *Dhammapada*, p. 38.)

142. Buddhism—so often labelled pessimistic—is striking in the genial attitude it takes towards asceticism. It encourages fasting only as a means to self-control and concentration of mind : for the rest the only kind of fasting it urges is " fasting from sin." Even the " man of the world " may be a true " Brahmin "—though it is very difficult. (*Cf.* Asoka's Minor Rock Edict, I : " Even by the small man, who chooses to exert himself, immense heavenly bliss may be won.")

The *Samana :* lit. " the calmed " (see note on 264).

144. By *faith* Buddhism means the calm acceptance of all Gautama taught : after his death it ceased to be an attitude to his person and became a conviction that his claims to omniscience were well founded, and that his system is the true interpretation of the world and of human life.

But Buddhism is nothing if not psychological, and faith (*saddha*) came to mean a subjective state of consciousness akin to serenity (*passadhi*), consequent upon acceptance of Buddha's teaching.

146. Fire is for the Buddhist the synonym of suffering : all is regarded as a flux—the world dissolving " with fervent heat." There is no meaning or permanence in this world : all the more need to seek salvation. In the burning heat of India the metaphor is a very vivid one for weariness and pain.

147-51. The Body too is a poor thing : in these ways Buddhism is distinctly pessimistic as compared with Christianity, which sees in the world a potential Kingdom of God, and in the human body a " temple of the Holy Spirit " : yet, be it noted, Gautama painted this lurid picture with intent to awaken men to the powers of their mind and character.

150. *A citadel of bones.* There are occasional gleams of grim humour in the Buddhist books : the following story illustrates both the " law of apperception " and the Buddhist attitude to the body. The hermit Mahā-Tissa was walking near Anuradhapura meditating upon the transiency of life. A woman who had quarrelled with her husband passed him, gaily dressed and bejewelled, and smiled at him, showing her pearly teeth. When the husband, who was in pursuit, came up with him he called to him : " Reverend Sir, did you see a woman pass this way ? " " I saw only a skeleton," replied the sage; " whether it was man or woman I know not " (Visuddhi-Maggai).

151. *Cf.* " My words shall never pass away."

152. *Like the ox.* So the prophet Amos addresses the fat and sensual women of his day : " Ye kine of Bashan " (Amos iv, 1) : " massive in body but small in mind " (*cf.* Deut. xxxii, 15).

153, 154. These famous words are held by Buddhists to have been those uttered by Gautama at the moment of enlightenment.

The allegory that underlies them is this : The Builder is Desire (Tanhā) the cause of rebirth : the seeker tried long to find this cause ; at the moment of his enlightenment it flashed into his mind, " If desire be dead, then there is nothing to bind man to the wheel of existence." The Builder causes the body to be built : its " corner-stone " (or ridge-pole) is ignorance (*avijjā*), and its " beams " are bad states of consciousness.

Admirably rendered by Sir Edwin Arnold :

> " Many a house of life
> Hath held me—seeking ever him who wrought
> These prisons of the senses, sorrow-fraught ;
> Sore was my ceaseless strife.
> But now,
> Thou Builder of this tabernacle—Thou !

I know Thee ! Never shall Thou build again
These walls of pain,
Nor raise the roof-tree of deceits ; nor lay
Fresh rafters on the clay ;
Broken Thy house is, and the ridge-pole split !
Delusion fashioned it !
Safe pass I them—deliverance to obtain."

155. *Cf.* "Like a pelican of the wilderness " (Ps. cii, 6).

157. This is a practice enjoined in the Books : the passage may mean also "for one of the three periods of life."

158. *Cf.* Matt. vii, 1–5 : "Judge not, that ye be not judged," etc.

164. *Bears fruit* . . . It dies down after flowering.

166. The hedonistic note in Buddhism cannot be denied : " Ethics," says Dr. Martineau, "must either perfect themselves in religion, or disintegrate themselves in hedonism." Buddhist ethics, seeing no great social purpose being worked out in the world, fails to reconcile the claims of self-culture and benevolence, falling back upon the monastic compromise that in the long run self-culture is the highest benevolence. (*Cf.* Introduction, p. 14)

171. It *looks* gay and splendid : it *is* an engine of destruction ; it is treacherous as a morass.

174. *Cf.* Matt. vii, 14 : "Narrow is the way which leadeth unto life, and few there be that find it."
Ps. cxxiv, 7 : "Our soul is escaped as a bird out of the snare of the fowler."

175. The East has always held that holy living gives miraculous power. Arahats were said to possess this power (*jddhi*) of flying through the air, or "levitation." There are still Hindus who claim these powers : but southern Buddhism does not take them seriously. I asked several Buddhists if this power were now attainable. "Possibly in Thibet," they answered.*

176. *Cf.* Jas. ii, 10 : "Whosoever shall keep the whole

* " *The Buddhist*," vol. i, No. 9, contains an account by an eye-witness of a self-levitated lāma.

law, and yet stumble in one point, he is become guilty of all."
But the underlying idea in St. James, of loyalty to the
King, is of course not present to the Buddhist mind.

178. *Universal empire :* the height of worldly ambition.

Conversion : i.e. the first step towards Nirvāna, when
the attention is fixed upon the Supreme Bliss. "*Sotāpatti* "
means "entering the stream," up which the convert has
to forge his way. After this ethical change he may have
to undergo seven more births before he attains the goal.

182. The Buddha, being free of all taints or germs of
rebirth, has no crack in his armour through which he may
be wounded : *i.e.* he has no cause of rebirth.

183. The ideal is not, as is often said, merely negative :
it is also positive and inward. *Cf.* St. Paul's more emphatic
words : "*Abhor* that which is evil, *cleave to* that which is
good " (Rom. xii, 9).

The Buddhas. According to the Books there are many
Buddhas : some in the dim past, others in the distant future.
In Ceylon, Buddhists look wistfully for the coming Buddha
—*Metteyya* or *Maitri*—the Loving One. In Japan they
worship *Amida* Buddha—an ideal.

184. The word translated "fortitude " is "*kantibalam*,"
patience-strength, that blending of great qualities, passive
and active, Eastern and Western, which is as rare as it is
beautiful.

194. *Cf.* Ps. cxxiii, 1 : "Behold how good and pleasant it
is for brethren to dwell together in unity."

197–200. This section may be regarded as the Buddhist,
analogue of the Beatitudes of Christ : it depicts the blessed
life as a life of calm and peace ; either solitary or in the
company of Buddha's true followers, a man may enjoy that
bliss which is the bloom upon virtue in this life : and hereafter the Rest of the Ineffable.

207. Like Jesus, Gautama offers his followers a family life
whose ties are more intimate and tender than those of blood.
In the Sangha they are to find their kinsfolk and a better
family life than they have left. [*Cf.* "Who is My mother

or My brethren ? . . . Whosoever shall do the will of God, the same is My brother and My sister and mother."—Mark iii, 35.] Yet it must be borne in mind that to enter this company a man must be a celibate: and that perfect solitude is held up as the safer ideal.

208. The cold clear moonlight of this simile is symbolic of the Buddhist ideal.

212, 213. Buddhism teaches benevolence to all, attachment to none. It is a monastic ideal, and may be paralleled from such books as the *Imitatio Christi*. *Cf.* Bk. I, chap. viii: "We must have charity towards all, but familiarity is not expedient."

There is, however, a vital difference: the Buddhist Bhikkhu is to shun society that nothing may mar his self-culture: the Christian monk that he may be "familiar with God alone, and with His Angels." When Prince Siddhartha (afterwards the Buddha) heard of the birth of his son Rahula, and they tried to bring him back, he is said to have remarked: "That is one more bond to be cut." The "Great Renunciation" involved no less than this.

218. *The Ineffable*. The Buddha describes Nirvāna probably from his own experience of that ecstatic joy which is said to be the reward of deep meditation.

This word "ineffable" is one used all by who have known this experience. *Cf.* Myers' *St. Paul*:

> "Oh could I tell, ye surely would believe it !
> Oh could I only say what I have seen !
> How should I tell, or how can ye receive it,
> How till He bringeth you where I have been ? "

and St. Paul's words of his own experience in 2 Cor. xii, 2–4.

Against the stream. The fight for character is one against long odds. Nature has at times to be "pitchforked." (*Cf.* Mrs. Rhys Davids' *Buddhist Psychology*, p. lxvii.) Man is not at the mercy of the "stream" of natural impulse; but swimming against it is hard work. (*Cf.* 244, 245.)

221. *Phenomenal existence :* Pali *namā rupa,* "name an form," *i.e.* things mental and material.

227. *Atula :* according to the Commentator, one (Gautama's disciples : he is not mentioned elsewhere.] we read " atulam " the meaning is " an incomparable saying.

241. *Disuse . . . mantras : i.e.* if the words are not use they are forgotten.

251. *Lust . . . hatred . . . folly.* The three inveterate foe of the good life. Buddhism sees that man has in him ap tiger, and ass. (*Cf.* Introduction, p. 15.)

252. Or " as the fowler hides his snare."

254, 255. We have followed the Sinhalese scholar, M James D'Alwis, in this translation : he is supported by tl Commentary. Another possible rendering is : " No or outside the Buddhist community can walk through the ai but only a samana " (Fausböll). But this taxes tl construction too severely, and as Professor Max Müll says, Buddha did not encourage the display of miraculou power.

264. *Cf. Imitatio Christi,* bk. I, chap. xvii : " The hab and the shaven crown do little profit : but change of manner and perfect mortification of passions make a true religiou man."

Samano, before Gautama's day, meant " ascetic," bein derived from the root " *sram* "—to work hard, to do penanc He gave a new derivation and a new significance to th word—*sam,* meaning " calm."

264-9. These stanzas contain a play on the words Gautama is giving new definitions of current terms. It hardly possible to render these in English : perhaps in 264- the use of the word " religious " as both noun and adjectiv is a fair analogy from Christian monasticism. The pun i 270 is only to be permitted as illustrating the spirit of tl section.

268-9. So Asoka says of impiety and piety : " The or course avails me for the present life, the other avails n also for the life to come." (Pillar Edict, III); and Thom à Kempis, quoting Phil. iii, 8: "He is truly prudent, that regards all earthly things as dung, that he may gain Christ."

270. Meekness is the true heroism: "Blessed are the meek, for they shall inherit the earth"; "Fight the good fight." As in mediaeval Europe, so in ancient India, all "nobles" (Aryans) were warriors. Gautama gives a new definition of the true knight. (*Cf.* the history of the words "chivalry," "gentle," and "generous," under Christian influences.)

273. *The four truths:* suffering: its cause: its cure: the eightfold path of escape.

The seer: cakkhumā, the man who has the eye for truth: the man of insight.

274. The "*seeing of Purity*." The phrase may mean equally well the "purification of vision." The man of insight is the pure man; to one who ventured to dispute Gautama's judgment he exclaimed: "Shall he whose mind is dominated by passion surpass the Blessed One in wisdom?" (*Cf.* Christ's words: "My judgment is just, because I seek not Mine own will.")

276. *Blessed Ones:* Tathāgatā, "those who have *arrived*," or reached Nirvāna.

277-9. "*All is passing*": one of the leading tenets of Heraclitus and the Orphists, who belong to the same century as the Buddha (sixth century B.C). Their teaching, so far as it has survived, has many points of similarity with his.

"*All is passing . . . all is sorrow . . . all is unreal.*" The words ring out again and again like the solemn tolling of some cloister bell, summoning men away from the pursuit of shadows, to that only worthy object "the path of Purity" —Nirvāna.

283. *Vanam* means either "lust" or a "forest": English cannot reproduce the play upon words.

284. Even married love is regarded by Buddhism as an "entanglement" of this kind.

7

286. *Cf.* the parable of the Rich Fool, and St. James: "Go to now, ye that say to-day or to-morrow we will go into the city, and spend a year there . . . whereas ye know not what shall be on the morrow" (iv, 13, 14).

294. The Commentator explains this curious verse as follows: The *Mother* is lust: the *Father* self-will: the *Kings* are heresies—two extremes on either side of the middle path (*cf.* Introductory Note, § xx); the *Kingdom* is sensuality (*cf.* 97).

295. The five roads are lust, hatred, disturbance of mind, sloth, and doubt.

301. The principal objects of meditation.

302. *Hard is the community life :* reading *samānasamvāso* with Max Müller and the Chinese version, instead of 'samānasamvāso (= asamānasamvāso) with Fausböll and the Sinhalese.

The wanderer in the world : i.e. the layman.

307. Suffering is the blight upon sin.

310. *Therefore* . . . *Cf.* the simple authority of the seventh commandment, "Thou shalt not commit adultery," and of Christ's words to the woman taken in adultery, "Go and sin no more."

311. "*Corruptio optimi pessima.*"

324. *Dhānapālako :* i.e. guardian of wealth.

340. *The streams :* sensations.

The creeper : passion.

344. The pun on the word *vanam* (forest and lust) is repeated here: "tangle" perhaps expresses both meanings.

353. Spoken, according to the Commentary, when the Buddha was on the way to Benares, and the Brahmin Upaka sceptically asked him who was his Teacher, and what the cause of his serenity and joy. Here Gautama claims omniscience: elsewhere he claims to be the *only* Teacher: "Non seulement Çākyamuni est source de verité, mais il est la source unique" (De la Vallée Poussin, *Bouddhisme*, p. 138). (*Cf.* Mahāvagga i, 6, 8.)

356-9. As weeds spoil a good harvest, so these passions

spoil the good harvest of character. Seed sown in clean soil is fruitful: so are gifts to the Noble.

370. The five bonds to be cut are egoism, doubt, false asceticism, lust, and hatred. The five to be left off are longing for higher states of birth, for still higher ones, self-will, want of purpose, and ignorance. The five to be taken are faith, manliness, mindfulness, deep meditation, and wisdom. (Commentary.)

" He who has crossed the flood " = Oghatinna.

Take five more. Man is destined to be yoked, if not by sin, then by duty. (*Cf.* " Whose service is perfect freedom.")

373. *Divine pleasure :* the joy of the unified will.

384. Meditation may be either special or general: *i.e.* upon any of the forty objects which lead to Samādhi, or upon the transiency, sorrow, and unreality of things.

For he knows . . . Cf. " Ye shall know the Truth, and the Truth shall make you free " (John viii, 32).

385. Lit. " In whom is found neither near bank nor far ": *i.e.* neither noticing external objects by attending to them, nor letting his desires go out to seek them. (Commentary.)

387. The face of the seer is said to shine.

388. Deriving *Brāhmano* from the root *vah*—or *bah*—to put away.

394. *Cf.* Luke xi, 39 ; Matt. xxiii, 27.

398. The cable is Dōsa, hatred ; the chain with its links is Tanhā, desire in all its forms ; the bolt is Mōha, infatuation, or folly.

395. This stanza seems to have a Brahminical origin: unless we lay all the stress on *meditating.*

405. *Fixed or moving creatures*, according to the Sinhalese Commentary, refers either to men or to animals. In a metaphorical sense, fixed creatures are Arahats, moving ones are common men. In a literal sense fixed creatures may be such things as molluscs.

ILLUSTRATIVE SAYINGS OF THE DISCIPLES OF THE BUDDHA

THE following are selections from another book which bears the impress of a very early date, and gives us vivid glimpses of the Buddhist Ideal: the Thera-Therī-Gāthā, or Songs of the Elders and Sisters. *The Psalms of the Sisters*, Mrs. Rhys Davids' fine translation of the latter portion of this book, is a valuable commentary on the Dhammapada, and reveals the great power of Buddhism (whilst the enthusiasm for Buddha was still alive) over the human heart.

SAYINGS ILLUSTRATIVE OF THE BUDDHIST IDEAL

Its asceticism :

"Gold-bedecked and bejewelled, carrying her son upon her hip and followed by attendants, came my wife.

"Beholding her, the mother of my son, I beheld a snare set by the Evil One [Mara]." *Thera-gāthā*, 299.

"Where a man dwells alone, he is as Brahma ; where two dwell, they dwell as gods ; where three dwell, it is as a village ; where there are more, it is a rabble." (The fewer the safer !)
Ibid., 245.

Its stoicism :

"The rain pours gurgling down : alone dwell I in dreadful cave. Yet for me it holds not dread nor fear ; I am one who knows them not." *Ibid.*, 189.

"As the elephant calmly endures the battle, so this lean one, with limbs gnarled as tree-trunks, endures the sting of insects as he bathes." *Ibid.*, 243.

"The cold dark nights of winter chap the skin and freeze the thoughts, O Mogharāja! What shall the Bhikkhu do ?
"The men of Māgadha have taken in their harvest. I, too, like others who delight in life, will lie down and take my rest in the straw."

> "Home have I left ; for I have left my world!
> Child have I left, and all my cherished herds!
> Lust have I left, and Ill-will too is gone,
> And Ignorance have I put far from me ;
> Craving and root of craving overpowered,
> Cool am I now, knowing Nibbāna's peace."
> *Therī-gāthā*, 18.
> (MRS. RHYS DAVIDS' Translation.)

Its earnestness :

"Not for sleep is the star-spangled night, but for work to him who is wise." *Thera-gāthā*, 192.

"When disease assailed my body, then my mind awoke and cried, 'The sickness is upon me! It is high time to play the man.'" *Ibid.*, 30.

"Happy freedom! Happy freedom! Good it is to be freed from three crooked things, from scythe and plough and hoe. There they stand ; no use have I for them! Let me meditate again and again ; let me lead the strenuous life [of thought]." *Ibid.*, 43.

"Of yore my mind would wander whither caprice and desire led it. To-day I hold it in check as the mahout can hold with his prod the elephant in rut." *Ibid.*, 76.

"They who have lost their foothold fall. But they can, if they will, arise again and yet again. I have won up the steep slope : loving what is lovely I have easily attained." *Ibid.*, 62.

APPENDIX

THE BUDDHIST IDEAL

(ARAHATSHIP OR NIRVĀNA)

AS DEPICTED IN THE DHAMMAPADA

THE "ambrosial [or deathless] path," Nirvāna, is the prize which these stanzas hold out to the strenuous : this is at once the goal of effort and its cessation, a calm haven after strenuous voyaging.* The seer speaks with a quiet rapture and a serene assurance which convince us as we read, that whether it is Gautama himself who speaks, or whether it is the collective voice of his followers, here is in any case the utterance of a real experience of the soul. Can it be that these men entered behind the veil of sense and time, and that their voices ring down the ages from that mysterious Beyond to which the mystics of all ages have aspired ?

We cannot say ; yet it is very clear that if the metaphysical Nirvāna is a fantasy, the ethical Nirvāna is real enough : and Gautama was above all things an ethical teacher. That

---

* *Upasama* implies both the idea of Peace and the idea that there has been a struggle to win it.

we shall understand Nirvāna from a perusal of those pages is not likely; that it will attract Western thinkers is not wholly to be desired; but we can at least study the ethical experience of which Nirvāna is but the description and the attempted explanation: and a grasp of what Arahatship means is essential to the understanding of Buddhism. The Arahat is one who, through obedience to the preaching of Buddha, has reached that calm state when the will no longer struggles, but is unified and at rest.

As the eagle, after long strain of upward flight, stays poised in mid-air, so the seer reaches the calm and severe heights of character. This is Nirvāna in the present world: and Nirvāna hereafter may be more mysterious, but it must be of the same kind.

Very much as the Christian, experiencing " the peace that passes understanding," interprets in the light of this experience the serenity and calm of the Hereafter, so the Buddhist " saint," having known the quiet and serenity of the unified will, projects this experience into the future.

To both alike this future is "ineffably sublime "; words fail men when they attempt to speak of the Beyond: and yet we can piece together a picture of their inmost thoughts from such fragmentary descriptions of their experience as they let fall.

Arahatship and Nirvāna, then, form one ideal, and it is with this that the Dhammapada is concerned.

We have seen that Nirvāna is ineffable (stanza 218 and note); but we have also to remember that it can be experienced here and now. In stanza 402 we read:

"He is the Brahmin who in this very world knows the end of sorrow, who has laid the burden aside and is free." *

For whilst "the burden" is ultimately bodily existence, yet it is the sinfulness and egoism and pride of the flesh which make that burden so intolerable : the body is in fact a good servant but a bad master, and he who masters his body is already as it were freed from it.

"Happy is he," says the Dīgha Nikāya, "who is free of lust and beyond its power : the highest bliss is freedom from pride and self-will."
"There is no sorrow like existence, no bliss like Nirvāna," says the Dhammapada.
" 'The flesh lusteth against the spirit, and the spirit against the flesh,' cries St. Paul. . . . 'Unhappy man that I am! Who shall deliver me from this body of death?' "

These and similar passages are a cry for deliverance ; and both teachers insist upon the same great truth, that man's bodily life, in so far as it is dominated by self-will and lust, is an evil

* cf. stanza 32 : where "near to Nirvāna" should probably be rendered "in the very presence of Nirvāna." (RHYS DAVIDS.)

to be escaped at any cost.   Neither is Manichean :
it is not the body that is evil, but the body
enslaved by the tyranny of evil desires.

And for both teachers it is the perversity of
the " flesh " that shapes the ideal of escape ;
though the one longs after the life of dissolution,
and the other believes that he will be " clothed
upon " with a " glorified body " hereafter.*

The salient feature of the Buddhist ideal is
freedom :

> " Him I call Brahmin who has cut the bonds, who thirsts
> not for pleasure, who has left behind the hindrances."
> (See 397 and note on 398.)

The phrase "highest freedom" occurs more
than once in these stanzas as a synonym for
Nirvāna, and, as Mrs. Rhys Davids has shown,
it is this aspect of Nirvāna which is most frequently hymned in the *Psalms of the Sisters*,
that remarkable collection of verses attributed
to the women-elders of the Sangha.† (*Cf.*
Dhammapada, 90, 92, 93, 96, etc.)

Inasmuch as this "highest freedom" is
escape from lust and other "bonds," it is an

---

* From a more positive point of view we may say that
for the Buddhist, Peace is an ideal of equilibrium now and
of unconsciousness hereafter : for the Christian, Peace is
an ideal of conscious fellowship with God begun now and
hereafter consummated.

† This collection, published by the Pali Text Society, will
go far to prove how real and deep was the ethical experience
of the early Buddhists.

ideal for this life : inasmuch as it is escape from the round of rebirths it is an ideal for the future : here Arahatship passes over into Nirvāna.*

And in both alike the way of escape lies in the mind of man :

> "All that we are by Mind is wrought,
> Fashioned and fathered by our Thought." *

The Arahat has mastered his mind (that "frail and fickle thing" that in the worldling "leaps hither and thither, like a monkey seeking fruit) "; and therefore he is already free from the tyranny of the flesh (cf. 89). For it is the mental " bonds " —lust, pride, self-will—which have bound him through the long waste of years to one body after another; and it is "knowledge" which sets him free :

> "He is the Brahmin indeed who . . . has reached the end of rebirths, the sage whose knowledge is perfect, and who is perfect with all perfection."

This freedom of Nirvāna is envisaged as Rest : and there is in these stanzas a cry for rest which runs through all the Buddhist books like some pathetic fugue : a desire so passionate as to be almost unintelligible to Western minds.

But to men obsessed heart and spirit with the

---

* In technical phraseology the *ethical* Nirvāna is called Savupādisesanibbānam, or Nirvāna, in which the five skandhas or elements of being remain ; and the *metaphysical* Nirvāna is called Anupādisesanibbanam, or Nirvāna, in which they cease to exist. (See Note at end.)

" weary weight of the intolerable years," life after life of suffering and care, it is a real longing which here finds rhythmic expression ;

"All is fleeting, all is unreal, all is sorrowful." (277-9.)
"There is no sorrow, like to existence : no bliss like Nirvāna, the Supreme Rest." (202.)

Worldly existence is wholly evil ; but every man is free to cultivate the " otherworldly " frame of mind, and be at peace. For Buddhism is in a sense eudaemonistic ; it does not flout man's desire to be happy : only it defines this happiness in terms of inward peace and self-control.

Section XV of the Dhammapada is the Buddhist analogue of the Beatitudes of Jesus, and, as an ideal of the Happy Life, ranks high indeed.

It is an ideal of kindliness and serenity, of peace and unity, which is very winsome : it would be hard to pick a quarrel with the exponents of such a life !

To the Christian it seems none the less an ideal more passive and stoical, less loving and mystical than that of Jesus ; and yet we cannot but rejoice that the East has had this ideal so long before it. To the Karma-haunted millions of India it has shone with a steady and alluring radiance, in time past more potent than to-day, but even now embedded in their subconsciousness.

Its calm and cool attractiveness is beautifully

symbolised in the poetic imagery of the Dhammapada :

"The good man shines like the moon escaped from clouds,
he is pure as some unruffled lake." (95.)

And the company of such a leader with his
disciples is

"As the moon following the path of the stars." (208.)

·· Another lovely moonlit scene embodies and
symbolises the spirit of this ideal :

The Buddha's six chief disciples are in a
park, and as they sit in the tropical moonlight
they ask one another what quality in the Bhikkhu
could add to the beauty of the scene. Amongst
the answers are three which throw light upon
the meaning of Arahatship :

"The peace and insight of moral victory," says one,
"The joy and insight of Emancipation," says another ;

and Sāriputta wins the Master's approval by his
reply :

"When a Bhikkhu masters his heart [*cittam*] and does not
let it master him."

"Hear from me," says Gautama. "Hear from
me what kind of Bhikkhu could add a lustre to
the wood ; one who, sitting serene and controlled,
resolves : 'Till my heart is freed from the ferments
of lust I shall not quit my seat.' "*

This scene is most suggestive, for it throws

* Majjhima Nikāya, 32.

into strong contrast Buddhist and Christian Ethics, and further it leads us into the heart of a vexed and difficult problem.

With regard to the first point, it is sufficient to say here that Buddhism teaches a rigorous and calm self-mastery, Christianity demands a passionate self-surrender.

With regard to the second, we may state the problem thus : Is Nirvāna a social ideal ? Or is it an ideal of solitude and forgetfulness ? The answer seems to be that Buddhism holds out no promise of the reunion of emancipated "souls "; Nirvāna is the cessation of all personal existence : yet the experience of the peace and joy of Noble Companionship—such companionship and communion of soul as is here depicted—is too good not to be desired. And this desire has tinged the ideal picture of the Beyond : in spite of metaphysics the ethical asserts itself ;

" Good is the Vision of the Noble " (*i.e.* Arahats).
" Good is their company." (206.)

" A loyal friend is the truest kinsman :
Nirvāna is the greatest Bliss." (204.)

To sum up the Buddhist position upon the question of " Society and Solitude " is no easy task ; but we may express it tentatively thus : At first solitude is essential ;

" Alone man lives like Brahma : in twos men live like gods : in threes they are as a village. More than this is a mob."

And as the Dhammapada says,

> "Even for great benefit to another let no man imperil his own benefit." (166.)

But if an Arahat is to be found, his society can do nothing but good : let the Bhikkhu resort to him. If there are a company of Arahats, let them rejoice in communion and fellowship. And hereafter

> Nirvāna is "the unknown shore." (323.)
> It is "the solitude which it is hard to love." (88.)

With all his kindliness and even geniality Buddha does not disguise the fact that victory will be purchased at a heavy cost :

> "One is the road leading to wealth : another is that leading to Nirvāna."

To win to the goal will mean asceticism all along the line :

> "Cut out the bonds. . . .
> Play the man. . . .
> Travel stoutly alone. . . ."

Such are his rallying-cries.

For the "Path of Safety" is beset with "evil beasts." And to win across "the torrent" to the safety of the "other side" needs courage and strenuous effort. And, having won through, men will find a great solitude, a peace, a freedom, only to be purchased by ceasing to be. Such is Nirvāna in the fullest sense.

Freedom ; Safety ; Rest ; Calmness ; Kindli-

ness ; Self-control ҉ Solitary effort or the company
of the select few.   Above all, Bliss, ineffable yet
traceable to its seat in the unified will.   Such is
Arahatship, or Nirvāna in this present life.
It is a lofty ideal, and though no Buddhist
now strives to realise Nirvāna, yet there are men
in all Buddhist lands gazing into the remote
future to see Arahatship shining afar off like
some dim yet lovely star.   And because it
is ethical, therefore it is attainable :

> "I ought, therefore I can."

In the days of Gautama it is clear that men
reached the goal of Arahatship, and knew the
peace and joy of a mind and conscience at rest.
For the contagion of his enthusiasm and the
magnetism of his personality went far to energise
ideals which are real enough beneath a tropic
sun, and, in so far as they are ethical ideals,
vital enough in all lands.   And to-day Buddhists
look wistfully to a Coming One, Maitri, who
shall spur them on to victory : or they put
their trust in the grace of an Amida who demands
only faith in his saving power.

The Christian will see in these aspirations
and yearnings the promise of a speedy fulfilment,
when men see the Majesty and the Love of God
revealed in Christ : and he will welcome the
teachings of Gautama the Buddha as the utterance
of a prophet and a seer.

NOTE

Nirvāna is thus explained in the Abhi-dhammattha-Sangaha, translated by Mr. Shwe Zan Aung, and published by the Pali Text Society under the title *Compendium of Philosophy.*

OF NIBBĀNA

˙ Now Nibbāna, which is reckoned as beyond these worlds, is to be realised through the knowledge belonging to the Four Paths. It is the object of those Paths, and of their Fruits. It is called Nibbāna, in that it is a " departure " from that craving which is called Vāna, lusting. This Nibbāna is in its nature single, but for purposes of logical treatment it is twofold, namely, the element of Nibbāna, wherewith is yet remaining stuff of life, and the element without that remainder. So, too, when divided into modes, it is threefold—namely, Void, Signless, and Absolute Content.

MNEMONIC

Great Seers, wholly from Vāna—lust set free,
Declare Nibbāna such a path to be :—
Past death, past end (it goes, this blessed way),
Uncauséd, having no beyond, they say.

Thus, as fourfold, Tathāgatas reveal,
The ultimate kinds of things we know and feel :—
Mind first, and next, concomitants of mind,
Body as third, Nibbāna last in kind.

www.ingramcontent.com/pod-product-compliance
Lightning Source LLC
Chambersburg PA
CBHW021149090426
42740CB00008B/1021